D.J. TAYLOR

W0091175

GEORGE ORWELL

A Reader's Guide

YALE UNIVERSITY PRESS
NEW HAVEN AND LONDON

Copyright © 2024 D.J. Taylor

Published in paperback in 2025. First published in hardback in 2024 as *Who Is Big Brother: A Reader's Guide to George Orwell*

For information about this and other Yale University Press publications, please contact:
U.S. Office: sales.press@yale.edu   yalebooks.com
Europe Office: sales@yaleup.co.uk   yalebooks.co.uk

Set in Adobe Caslon Pro by IDSUK (DataConnection) Ltd
Printed in Denmark By Nørhaven A/S, Viborg

Library of Congress Control Number: 2023951044

A catalogue record for this book is available from the British Library.
Authorized Representative in the EU: Easy Access System Europe, Mustamäe tee 50, 10621 Tallinn, Estonia, gpsr.requests@easproject.com

ISBN 978-0-300-27298-7 (hbk)
ISBN 978-0-300-28423-2 (pbk)

10 9 8 7 6 5 4 3 2 1

GEORGE ORWELL: A READER'S GUIDE

D.J. Taylor is an award-winning novelist, critic and biographer. His book *Orwell: The Life* won the 2003 Whitbread Prize for Biography, and *Orwell: The New Life* was published in 2023. His books include two Booker-longlisted novels and a life of Thackeray.

OTHER BOOKS BY D. J. TAYLOR

FICTION

Great Eastern Land
Real Life
English Settlement
After Bathing at Baxter's: Stories
Trespass
The Comedy Man
Kept: A Victorian Mystery
Ask Alice
At the Chime of a City Clock
Derby Day: A Victorian Mystery
Secondhand Daylight
The Windsor Faction
From the Heart (Amazon Kindle Single)
Wrote for Luck: Stories
Rock and Roll is Life
Stewkey Blues: Stories
Flame Music

NON-FICTION

A Vain Conceit: British Fiction in the 1980s
Other People: Portraits from the Nineties (with Marcus Berkmann)
After the War: The Novel and England Since 1945
Thackeray
Orwell: The Life
On the Corinthian Spirit: The Decline of Amateurism in Sport
Bright Young People: The Rise and Fall of a Generation 1918–1940
What You Didn't Miss: A Book of Literary Parodies
The Prose Factory: Literary Life in England Since 1918
The New Book of Snobs
Lost Girls: Love, War and Literature 1939–1951
On Nineteen Eighty-Four: A Biography
Critic at Large: Essays and Reviews 2010–2022
Orwell: The New Life

E.A.C.T. (1932–2022)
In fond memory

Orwell is one of those writers you can never quite get away from. I do not just mean that the stream of books and articles about him seems inescapable, so that any intellectuals who may submit to having a list of their heroes wrung from them are likely to put him in the first two or three whatever their age . . . whatever their other preferences and – more oddly at first sight – whatever their political affiliations, if any. And if they have none, incidentally, this is as much Orwell's doing as anyone else's. However: Orwell is hard to get away from because no view of him can ever be final.

—Kingsley Amis

No novelist has more than a few stories to tell. They are the myths of life which each novelist creates for himself.

—Anthony Powell

CONTENTS

ILLUSTRATIONS

Orwell and his adopted son Richard, Islington, 1946.

INTRODUCTION: MAPPING THE TERRITORY

Of the making of books about George Orwell there is apparently no end. The year 2023 alone brought a new biography – to add to the half-dozen that already exist: an examination of Orwell's relationship with Russia, a study of his first wife, and a highly detailed gazetteer of his haunts and homes. And all this is to ignore what might be called Orwell projections, the novels that update *Animal Farm* or re-imagine *Nineteen Eighty-Four* from Julia's point of view. With so many bookshop display tables groaning under the weight of Orwell-iana, what is the point of adding to it? One answer is that there is always something new to say about Orwell: however tightly meshed the net flung out to pinion him, he has a gratifying habit of slipping through the cracks. Another is the fact that Orwell Studies is becoming increasingly specialised, a matter of Orwell's dealings with empire, Jewishness, the working classes, America and many other coigns of vantage besides. A third is personal. I have been writing about Orwell, on and off, for over twenty years and still there are avenues of his life and work that don't seem to me to have been adequately explored – avenues, more to the point, that don't necessarily lend themselves to the standard biographical or critical approaches. What follows, consequently, is intended to be both straightforward and oblique: a book that (I hope) will appeal to readers who have only just become aware of Orwell, and also to Orwell diehards who have spent long years in pursuit of his intoxicating scent.

But first some basic information. George Orwell, whose real name was Eric Arthur Blair, came into the world on 25 June 1903 in Motihari, Bengal. He disliked being called Eric, on the grounds that it reminded him of a pious Victorian children's book by Dean Farrar entitled *Eric, or Little by Little* (1885), and once complained to his friend Rayner Heppenstall that 'People always grow up like their names. It took me nearly thirty years to work off the effects of being called Eric.' The Blairs were essentially a colonial family: Richard Walmesley Blair, Orwell's father, worked for the Indian Civil Service; his mother, Ida Mabel (*née* Limouzin), came from a clan of French shipbuilders who had migrated to Burma. There were two sisters, Marjorie, born in 1898, and Avril, Orwell's junior by five years, with whom he lived on affectionate but undemonstrative terms.

Orwell was born with defective bronchial tubes, foreshadowing the ill health from which he suffered throughout his life. A diary kept by his mother in 1905 after the family's return to England (Mr Blair remained in India) is largely a chronicle of her son's ailments. He was a clever, studious boy who, after five years at St Cyprian's, a fashionable south-coast preparatory school, won a King's Scholarship to Eton. Most teenagers of his ability and social class would have proceeded to Oxford or Cambridge, but despite well-attested literary interests Orwell seems to have idled away his adolescence. He left Eton shortly before Christmas 1921 and the following autumn, at the age of nineteen, departed for Burma and a job in the imperial police force.

Little is known of Orwell's four and a half years in the East. Returning to England in 1927 on a medical certificate – he had been suffering from dengue fever – he shortly afterwards announced to his startled family that he intended to become a writer. Progress was slow, and it was not until January 1933 that the firm of Victor Gollancz published his first book, a record of his tramping adventures and an eighteen-month stint in France entitled *Down and Out in Paris and London*. He was frequently hard up, had no fixed base and was often reduced to staying at his parents' house in Southwold, Suffolk. Although Orwell earned very little from his early work, his output in these formative days was prodigious: in the next six years he produced four novels (*Burmese Days*, *A Clergyman's Daughter*, *Keep the Aspidistra Flying* and *Coming Up for Air*) and two works of non-fiction, *The Road to Wigan Pier* (1937), an account of his visit to the 'distressed areas' of the north of England, and *Homage to Catalonia* (1938), a memoir of six months spent fighting on the Republican side in the Spanish Civil War, during which he was shot through the throat by a fascist sniper.

Orwell had married his first wife, Eileen O'Shaughnessy, in 1936; in the early years of their marriage the couple inhabited a remote Hertfordshire cottage. The experience of serving in Spain left him with an enthusiasm for the radical politics he had witnessed in revolutionary Barcelona and a thoroughgoing contempt for Soviet interference in the war. Spain had also further undermined his health: he almost died of a tubercular haemorrhage early in 1938 and was forced to spend nearly a year on the sidelines, at first recuperating in a sanatorium and then convalescing in Morocco on a trip underwritten by a wealthy admirer. Having joined the Independent Labour Party in 1938 and adopted its pacifist stance towards the prospect of European conflict, he underwent a Damascene conversion in August 1939 after hearing news of the Russo-German pact: 'I would give my life for England readily enough if I thought it necessary,' runs a diary entry from August 1940.

But war work proved difficult to acquire. He was graded unfit for military service and it was not until the summer of 1941 that he secured a post as a talks producer in the Eastern Service of the BBC, commissioning and taking part in broadcasts to India and other imperial possessions threatened by the Japanese armies. Although he believed that he had wasted his time at the BBC, the evidence suggests that he worked hard and was responsible for some innovative programming, notably the poetry feature *Voice*. He was much happier at the left-wing weekly magazine *Tribune*, to which he moved in November 1943, acting as literary editor and contributing a regular column entitled 'As I Please'. He was already at work on *Animal Farm*, his coruscating satire of the Russian Revolution, although wartime publishing delays (and the intervention of a Soviet spy in the Ministry of Information) meant that the novel was not published until August 1945.

Animal Farm was an immediate success which both made Orwell's reputation and offered him the prospect of financial security. But his personal life was in disarray. Eileen, whose health was arguably as poor as his own, had died unexpectedly in March 1945, leaving her widower in charge of a ten-month-old baby, christened Richard Horatio Blair, whom the couple had adopted the previous year. Though clearly ailing – he had another serious haemorrhage early in 1946 – Orwell resolved to bring up the child himself. He spent much of the remaining four years of his life on the Inner Hebridean island of Jura, working on his final novel, *Nineteen Eighty-Four*. This chilling dystopia, published in June 1949, was an international sensation. By this time Orwell was gravely ill. After a period in a Cotswold sanatorium he was transferred to University College Hospital, London. He died there on 21 January 1950, at the age of forty-six, shortly after contracting a second marriage to Sonia Brownell, whom he had met when she worked for his friend Cyril Connolly's magazine *Horizon*, and who inherited the bulk of his estate.

◎

Orwell died young. At an age when most writers are barely getting into their stride, he was marooned on his deathbed, setting his affairs in order and ruefully acknowledging to friends that the money rolling in from *Nineteen Eighty-Four* was merely 'fairy gold'. Most of the ornaments of that spangled tribe of British novelists born in the decade between 1900 and 1910 – Graham Greene, Evelyn Waugh, Anthony Powell – would outlive him by several decades, and in the case of Powell (1905–2000), who has some claims to be regarded as the shrewdest expositor of what made Orwell tick, by over half a century. One of the reasons why Orwell features so extravagantly in late twentieth-century literary memoirs – see, for example, the long account of him in Powell's *Infants of the Spring* (1976) – is the tragedy of his early death. To old associates such as George Woodcock, Rayner Heppenstall and Tosco Fyvel – two of whom wrote full-length books about him – he is the great dead friend, the exemplary bygone presence taken all too soon, whose shadow hangs over the world he left behind and grows more considerable as each year succeeds the next.

This premature departure had several consequences for Orwell's reputation in the decades that followed. Most obviously, it meant that the process of sanctification which attends the afterlives of most major writers kicked in almost on the instant. To read the reactions of Orwell's friends to news of his death is instantly to become aware of the mythologising blanket that seems to have fallen over the deceased's head. Woodcock, then living in Vancouver and informed by a fellow guest at a party, remembered that 'a silence fell over the room, and I realised that this gentle, modest and angry man had already become a figure of world myth'. It was the same with the journalist Malcolm Muggeridge, who, returning home from Orwell's funeral and casting his eye over the file of newspaper obituaries, felt that he could see in them 'how the legend of a man is created'. Most literary reputations take years or sometimes decades to coalesce, need careful handling by their brokers, and even then are subject to fret, fracture and constant reassessment. Orwell's, on the other hand, seems to have been in place within a week of his passing.

If you wanted a symbol of Orwell's near-immediate installation in the pantheon of mid-twentieth-century Western literature, it could be found in the June 1950 issue of a highbrow magazine called the *World Review*. Its subject had been gone for only a matter of months, but here already are selections from his wartime notebooks, a memoir by Fyvel and half a dozen of the era's grand eminences – Bertrand Russell, Aldous Huxley, Stephen Spender – queuing up to pay tribute. Secker & Warburg, Orwell's publishers since a mid-1940s falling-out with the firm of Victor Gollancz, are 'glad to announce that they will be publishing in the autumn a new volume of Mr Orwell's essays entitled *Shooting an Elephant*', and are anxious to inform the public that none of the contents has appeared in volume form before. Arthur Koestler assures potential purchasers that no parable since *Gulliver's Travels* is 'equal in profundity and mordant satire to *Animal Farm*'. And all this chimes with the editorial comment on the war-era diaries: 'looking back on the events through Orwell's eyes, it is astonishing to see how right he was'. Four months dead, the author of *Nineteen Eighty-Four* is already being acclaimed as a prophet, a moral visionary and a fabulist to rank with Swift.

It was not simply Orwell's death in poignant circumstances – a novel on the bestseller lists, a newly married wife in mourning, an adopted son left fatherless – that produced this outpouring of acclaim. If he had died young, then in the context of his career as a writer, his success had come comparatively late. *Animal Farm* (1945), written in his late thirties, trailed a decade-and-a-half-long career of what was sometimes not much more than hackwork. Until he was forty his name was barely known beyond the fairly restricted and mostly literary circles in which he moved. In fact, it is worth asking how posterity might rank Orwell had he died sometime during the Second World War – been blown up in the doodlebug raid that destroyed his house in Kilburn in 1944, say, or succumbed to the kind of tubercular haemorrhage that nearly claimed him two years later. The chances are that he would be remembered as an interesting minor novelist in a slightly old-fashioned genre, an accomplished filer of down-market reportage and a promising essayist with a talent for the newly fashionable craft of literary sociology. As it was, *Animal*

Farm and *Nineteen Eighty-Four* established him as one of the most successful writers of his age, only for Orwell to blow a promising hand by leaving the world as soon as the task was accomplished. Or rather, to have played the most promising hand of all by dying almost at the moment that his fame was assured. In his absence, vats of ink have been expended on the question of 'What George would have thought' of the various crises of late twentieth- and early twenty-first-century power politics, but this is to miss the point. One of the reasons we esteem Orwell is that he is not here to advise us. You suspect that a real live pundit would carry much less clout.

◎

And all this is to ignore the noise of history rumbling on in the background. It was not just that Orwell died young having written two internationally successful novels, but that he did so on the cusp of an age in which his work would acquire an extraordinary political resonance. The final months of his life in the room at University College Hospital came at a time when many of the implications of the Cold War – a phrase he has a strong claim to have invented – were becoming uncomfortably clear. No two books, it might be said, were more important to the decades-long stand-off between the West and the Soviet Union and its satellites than *Animal Farm* and *Nineteen Eighty-Four*. Each found itself weaponised by the CIA for propaganda purposes, filmed, broadcast, translated and smuggled across the borders of East European countries whose democratically governments had been replaced by stooge regimes who took their orders from Moscow. Orwell, consequently, is everywhere in the cultural life of the 1950s, on television screens (the first BBC dramatisation of *Nineteen Eighty-Four* dates from 1954), in Hollywood (the first film version came in 1956), on prime-ministerial reading lists ('Found the P.M. absorbed in George Orwell's book, *1984*' runs an entry in the diary of Churchill's doctor, Lord Moran, from February 1953), in animated films (MGM's version of *Animal Farm* debuted in 1954), on dime-store shelves and in the consciousness of a new generation of up-and-coming literary voices. To take only the United Kingdom, Orwell's influence on the agglomeration of 1950s talent known as the Movement (Kingsley Amis, Philip Larkin, John Wain and others) was acknowledged by practically everyone who took part: 'Of all the writers who appeal to the post-war intelligentsia, he is far and away the most potent,' Amis declared in 1957. 'No modern writer has his air of passionately believing what he has to say and of being determined to say it as forcefully and simply as possible.'

Ubiquity; talismanic status; constant reinvention on stage and screen: from the angle of recent English literature, Orwell's instant elevation into the canon and his influence on the popular culture of his day are practically unique. Just as Orwell maintained in his essay 'Charles Dickens' that a comedian could go onto a variety hall stage and imitate one of Dickens's characters and have a fair chance of being recognised, so he himself created half a dozen phrases – 'Big Brother', 'Room 101' – that have taken up residence in the minds of people who have never read a line of one of his books. The incremental effect in the half-decade after his death was to transform him into an almost mythological figure, endlessly invoked to explain a political crisis, a collision of ideology or a sociological cause célèbre. One or two of Orwell's old friends might have sniffed at these constant appropriations, but most of them were uncomfortably aware that they were caught up in the process themselves, collaborators in the perpetuation of the Orwell myth. Rayner Heppenstall's *Four Absentees* (1960), for example, is highly sensitive to some of the snares lying in wait for the average memorialist. Heppenstall (1911–81) had shared a flat with Orwell in the 1930s, liked him as a man but, as a paid-up member of the experimental school of the 1930s, found his novels oddly old-fashioned. Ten years after Orwell's death, Heppenstall's attitude to the clouds of posthumous glory billowing over his old friend's head is curiously double-edged:

I was no party to a cult or to a dissident faction. To me, Orwell had been a man I knew. Though I liked *Animal Farm*, I had never taken much interest in his work. I could see what qualities of masochism and courage, desperate search for experience, over-simplification and true simplicity, commonsense and foolishness, tenderness and cruelty, were tending to make him a cult figure. There was to be a legend. I might as well help to make it complete.

Heppenstall's part in making the 'legend' complete was to include an epic account of the occasion, sometime in the autumn of 1935, on which, having come home drunk from a visit to the theatre, he was intercepted by Orwell on the staircase, tersely upbraided by him ('Bit thick you know ... This time of night ... Wake up the whole street ...'), punched on the nose, locked in a bedroom and finally assaulted with a shooting-stick. It is a terrific piece of writing, full of highly convincing detail about the way in which Orwell behaved under stress, and yet, in the end, undermined by the reader's suspicion that Heppenstall's interpretative dice are loaded, that he is bringing in information that would not have been available to him at the time and, in particular, framing Orwell in a context that comes straight out of *Nineteen Eighty-Four*. At one point, for example, Heppenstall claims to see in his aggressor's face 'a curious blend of fear and sadistic exalta-tion'. We are back in the Ministry of Love – in the 1920s Raj, too, for a couple of paragraphs later Heppenstall can be found complaining to the mutual friend at whose house he takes refuge that Orwell had 'interviewed him like a district commissioner'.

All this – Heppenstall's mythologising, Heppenstall's score-settling, Heppenstall's incidental glosses – gestures at a problem liable to afflict anybody trying to get to the heart of Orwell's world. This is the difficulty of establishing what his work looked like at the time it was written. *Nineteen Eighty-Four*'s extraordinary long-term success has always encouraged what might be called a teleological view of Orwell, in which the reader tracks back through the early books looking for marker-posts on the path to the final masterpiece. None of this is to deny that all of his six novels are connected by a single authenticating thread. However site-specific the landscapes of *Burmese Days* (1934), *A Clergyman's Daughter* (1935), *Keep the Aspidistra Flying* (1936) and *Coming Up for Air* (1939), each of them advertises what is essentially the same plot, in which an oppressed and increasingly fearful solitary conducts an unsuccessful rebellion against the system which is grinding them down. John Flory in *Burmese Days* ends up committing suicide; Dorothy Hare in *A Clergyman's Daughter* returns to the stasis of her father's rectory; Gordon Comstock in *Keep the Aspidistra Flying* succumbs to the embrace of the 'money-god', marries his pregnant girlfriend and resumes his job in advertising; George Bowling in *Coming Up for Air*, having wandered spectre-like over the terrain of his Oxfordshire childhood, sneaks back to the outer London suburb of West Bletchley and the company of his joyless wife. Winston Smith may live in a futurist dystopia, but his predicament is effectively the same: in a world ruled by malign exterior forces, his goal is autonomy, the cultivation of a tiny, unpoliced space in which, however artificially or temporarily, he can be himself. Even *Animal Farm*, with its (mostly) non-human cast, turns out to be about a revolution that fails – or rather a revolution so detached from its original moorings that it ceases to be a revolution at all.

Naturally, it is possible to overstress these continuities. If Orwell's early books are full of ghostly prefigurations – Gordon, for example, insisting that his poems are 'dead' because he inhabits a 'dead world' – then the patterns which connect *Keep the Aspidistra Flying* to *Nineteen Eighty-Four* can sometimes be exaggerated. Which is to say that, by and large, in the round and with due regard to Orwell's wider creative trajectory, the great majority of his work has a life of its own. It would be odd if it didn't, given the vast corpus of reportage, book, film and theatre reviews, weekly columns and casual journalism to which Orwell put his name during his twenty years or so as a writer. From the angle of the early twenty-first century, in which a Bookerwinning novelist might produce a new work only every two or three years, Orwell's output was simply prodigious: Peter Davison's monumental edition of his collected writings (*George Orwell: The Complete Works*, 1998) runs to twenty volumes, and this is to ignore the dozens of new letters that have come to light in the intervening quarter of a century. Almost every year of his professional life, when seen through the prism of his commission book, yields up an eye-catching file of statistics. In the first twenty months of the Second World War alone, as well as writing the long essay *The Lion and the Unicorn: Socialism and the English Genius* (1941), he managed to file 128 book reviews, thirty-eight theatre reviews and forty-three cinema reviews, which works out at a piece of journalism every three days.

Why did he write so much? On one level the sheer superabundance of Orwell's oeuvre is a consequence of the milieu in which he operated. It was an age in which authors – even very successful ones – were expected to be prolific. Graham Greene, for example, is thought to have written more than a thousand book reviews in the 1930s alongside the novels that made his name, while a skim through Donat Gallagher's edition of *The Essays, Articles and Reviews of Evelyn Waugh* (1983) reveals their author to have been – albeit intermittently – not much more than a high-class hack. In 'Why I Write' (1946), Orwell left a fascinating account of the various motives that drive people to put words on paper. They include 'sheer egoism', 'aesthetic enthusiasm', 'historical impulse' and 'political purpose' (significantly, Orwell is keen to use the adjective 'in the widest possible sense'), but most experienced Orwell-fanciers, having run an eye over the list, will suspect that one of the most pressing justifications for writing books and items of journalism has been omitted altogether. This, it is safe to conclude, is money. If it is not entirely accurate to say (as he once maintained) that he wrote *Keep the Aspidistra Flying* simply to get his hands on Victor Gollancz's £100 advance – there are other comments about his desire to create 'a work of art' – then for most of his life he was a jobbing writer, eager to accept the majority of the commissions that came his way and not averse to making compromises should the situation demand it. 'A poisonous paper,' he once remarked of a short-lived periodical named *Modern Youth* for which he was contracted to write at the very start of his career, 'but one has got to live.' To balance this matter-of-fact awareness of some of the practical realities of his craft is his consistent habit, later in life, of supplying pieces of journalism to obscure left-leaning periodicals of which he approved for no payment at all.

Elsewhere in 'Why I Write', Orwell is careful to note that he is not a propagandist pure and simple: life will always get in the way. 'So long as I remain alive and well I shall continue to feel strongly about prose style, to love the surface of the earth, and to take a pleasure in solid objects and scraps of useless information. It is no use trying to suppress that side of myself.' What this means in practice is that any page or two of his writing taken at random is almost certain to reveal a host of deep-rooted impulses and fixations quietly making their presence felt. There are times when the allusions on display are not much more than a private joke. *Nineteen Eighty-Four*, for example, contains a scene in which Winston Smith, awaiting interrogation at the Ministry of Love, watches a fellow detainee attempt to palm a piece of bread to the starving man who sits beside him. 'Bumstead!' roars the telescreen. '2713 Bumstead J! Let fall that piece of bread.' This is a reference to a man named Jack Bumstead, brother of the Southwold grocer with whom Orwell's parents had dealt in the 1930s and on whom Orwell had not set eyes for nearly ten years. In much the same way, *A Clergyman's Daughter* pokes some mild fun at a certain 'Dr Gaythorne' – Gathorne-Hardy being the family name of the local Suffolk magnate, the earl of Cranbrook, two of whose sons Orwell had known at Eton. Or there is the remark in *Burmese Days* about Flory's skin turning lemon-coloured in the tropical sun: a nod to a family joke from Orwell's childhood in which his mother's forebears the Limouzins were always known as 'the lemonskins'.

Seen in this light, most of Orwell's books and major essays reveal themselves as a series of complex puzzles for the reader to decipher: mosaics of allusion and hidden purpose. Some of them are links in the long associative chain that would eventually lead to *Animal Farm* and *Nineteen Eighty-Four*; others need thoroughgoing interpretation, carry us off into the innermost recesses of Orwell's private world and the influences to which he was subject. A private world, more to the point, which is full of subterfuge and exaggeration. It was Kingsley Amis (a fan) who once observed that 'Not until his fantasies have been exposed and discarded can we properly value the truths he told.' The aim of this book, consequently, is not to regard the Orwell canon as a kind of eternal golden braid in which every thread contributes to the overall design, but to ask some basic questions about how and why specific parts of it came to be written, the reasons why individual books and pieces of journalism arrived at their final shape, and why individual characters behave as they do. To take some examples: Gordon Comstock in *Keep the Aspidistra Flying* is a struggling poet, but what sort of poems does he write and how does he fit into the literary land-scape that Orwell devises for him? *Nineteen Eighty-Four* is a world built on the sophisticated use of surveillance technology, but how does that technology work and what, if anything, does Orwell know about the systems by which the rulers of Oceania keep their citizenry in order? *Animal Farm* turns the natural order of civilisation on its head by fashioning a society in which animals turn the tables on their human oppressors, but why is it that when Orwell has to select a species bent on betraying the revolution he should instantly settle on the pigs?

And then there is Big Brother, *Nineteen Eighty-Four*'s talismanic centrepiece and symbolic focus. Who is he? Where does he come from? Does he even exist, except as a face on a poster or an image on a screen? None of these questions is immediately soluble, but no discussion of what the novel is ultimately 'about' can fail to take them into account. 'A writer's work is not something he takes out of his brain like tins of soup out of a storeroom,' Orwell declared in a wartime essay about Henry Miller. 'He has to create it day by day out of his contacts with people and things.' How did Orwell set about this daily act of creation? Who were those 'people and things'? What influences was he subject to, and how do the books he wrote bring off their effects? What games was he playing beneath the surface of his texts? 'Good prose is like a windowpane,' Orwell once wrote. It is not one of his most convincing epigrams, but its relevance to Orwell's work can hardly be overstated. As a writer he intended his books to be transparent, instantly accessible to their audiences and conveying truths that no amount of counter-assertion could gainsay. At the same time his writing is full of secrets – tantalising glimpses of private histories, romantic chasms, psychological quirks and deep-rooted questions of upbringing, all of them calculated to take us closer to the man he was, and to the work – and the legend – he created.

Eric Blair aged three, in sailor suit.

1

HERITAGE

BURMESE DAYS • A CLERGYMAN'S DAUGHTER •
'RUDYARD KIPLING'

The date and location of Orwell's birth – two years after Queen Victoria's death and in the greatest of her imperial possessions – were vitally important to both the view he came to take of the world and the kind of person he imagined himself to be. The memory of his golden Edwardian childhood in the South Oxfordshire countryside dominated his imaginative life, and any contemporary writer who set out to recreate the vistas of the first decade of the twentieth century was sure of an approving review. Writing about Rosamond Lehmann's short story 'The Red-Haired Miss Daintreys' in 1940, for example, he notes that 'the peaceful, slumbrous atmosphere of the late Edwardian age is wonderfully evoked'. H.G. Wells, too, is regularly commended for, as his young devotee puts it, 'being able more than almost any other writer to make the sleepy years at the end of the last century and the beginning of this one seem a good time to be alive'.

Coming Up for Air (1939) preaches exactly the same lesson. George Bowling, its reminiscing hero, may be ten years older than his creator but his recapitulations of past time are quite as fervent as Orwell's nostalgia for the world inhabited by Lehmann's Miss Daintreys:

'1910, 1911, 1912 . . . I tell you,' he insists, 'it was a good time to be alive.' Undoubtedly, the elegiac note that Orwell brings to virtually every recollection he produces from his early life is coloured by an awareness of the conflagration of 1914–18 that would blow the safe, comfortable landscapes of Edwardian England to smithereens, but there is nothing contrived about his sorrowings over the vanished world of childhood: these are authentic memories, you feel, a series of solid, inalienable yardsticks next to which the landscapes of the post-war era can seem frighteningly insubstantial.

All the same, like many a product of the Edwardian age, Orwell would probably have conceded that the really crucial influences on him came from the decades that had preceded it. His first four novels were published in the 1930s, but their narrative line nearly always tracks back deep into the Victorian era. Gordon in *Keep the Aspidistra Flying* (1936) is the grandson of 'Granpa Comstock', a self-aggrandising nineteenth-century plutocrat who has crushed the life out of his timorous descendants to the point where it is suggested that the massive granite slab erected on his grave has been placed there with the express intention of ensuring that the deceased cannot get out from underneath. The Reverend Hare in *A Clergyman's Daughter* is a man born out of his time, fundamentally detached from the world of Ramsay MacDonald and Stanley Baldwin and much keener on remembering his undergraduate years at late Victorian Oxford than worrying about the attendance figures at his moribund Suffolk church. Some of George Bowling's earliest memories are of his father and his uncle arguing over the conduct of the Boer War, and the collective local judgement that 'Vicky was the best queen who'd ever lived.' In most of Orwell's work the Victorian age features as a kind of imaginative touchpaper, requiring only the tiniest spark to set it off. When he writes about Thackeray, or Dickens, or the great Victorian sporting novelist R.S. Surtees, there is an almost instantaneous sense of connection, the feeling that Orwell is at home in the world of *Nicholas Nickleby* or *A Shabby Genteel Story* in a way that he would not be in the milieu of a more modern novelist. His friend Cyril Connolly once pronounced that he was 'a revolutionary in love with 1910', but there is a way in which his gaze extends even further back than this to the landscapes of the 1860s and 1870s.

The past was always vividly alive to Orwell: its artefacts and its literature kept their hold on his imagination until the day he died. A recently discovered letter to his Suffolk girlfriend Eleanor Jaques from the early 1930s records a visit to the British Museum, where his eye alights on a glass pot from the early Roman era whose base is inscribed with the words *Felix fecit* ('Felix made this'). To Orwell this is 'extraordinarily moving', so much so that, as he told Eleanor, 'I seemed to see poor Felix's face just as though I had known him. I suppose he was a slave.' Not surprisingly, when he came to conceptualise the 2,000 years or so of English history that lay before the world into which he was born he did so entirely according to the *idées fixes* to which early twentieth-century English history was subject. There is a highly significant page or two towards the end of *A Clergyman's Daughter* describing the curriculum of the wretched private school in a west London suburb where Dorothy ends up teaching. The children are so sublimely ignorant that, asked when motor cars were invented, one of them solemnly replies, 'About a thousand years ago. By Columbus.' Until Dorothy's arrival her class has been taught out of a jingoistic textbook called *The Hundred Page History of Britain*, whose cover consists of a portrait of Boudicca draped in a Union Jack. Dorothy, naturally, is aghast:

History was the hardest thing to teach them. Dorothy had not realised until now how hard it is for children who come from poor homes to have even a conception of what history means. Every upper-class person, however ill informed, grows up with some notion of history; he can visualise a Roman centurion; an eighteenth-century nobleman; the terms Antiquity, Renaissance, Industrial Revolution evoke some meaning, even a confused one, in his mind. But these children came from bookless homes and from parents who would have laughed at the notion that the past has any meaning for the present. They had never heard of Robin Hood, never played at Cavaliers and Roundheads, never wondered who built the English churches or what Fid. Def. on a penny stands for.

And here most readers will have noticed a slippage in the narrative. Gradually Dorothy's view of the ignorami of Ringwood House recedes and Orwell's takes over. But his choice of the historical highlights of which these lower-middle-class children have never heard is rather significant. Another kind of writer might have selected Magna Carta, the Glorious Revolution of 1689 or the Reform Act of 1832. Orwell plumps for a medieval English outlaw whom centuries of mythologising have tended to detach from historical reality, the opposing sides in the English Civil War, the architectural foundation of native Christianity and the rubric that authenticates the idea of a state church. All this is enough to establish Orwell as a historical romantic, for whom the past is a kind of gigantic frieze picked out with legendary figures and mighty deeds. Tellingly, a year or two before this paragraph was written, when asked by a small boy he was tutoring which side he might have supported had he been alive in 1642, the embryonic socialist declared that he would have been a Cavalier on the grounds that the Roundheads were 'such dreary people'.

The same mental atmosphere can be detected in an 'As I Please' column he wrote early in 1947 for *Tribune*, inspired by a *Spectator* column in which the writer Harold Nicolson, 'consoling himself as best he could for having reached the age of sixty', had noted down some of the great events he had witnessed in the course of his life. As a one-time diplomat who had spent time in pre-Soviet Russia, Nicolson had seen the tsar surrounded by his bodyguard of Cossacks blessing the River Neva. Orwell admits that he cannot match this feat, but produces a list of celebrity sightings that includes the music hall legends Marie Lloyd and Little Tich, 'a whole string of crowned heads', the French Great War strategist and future Vichy leader Marshal Pétain and, finally, Queen Mary, the wife of King George V, glimpsed in the vicinity of Windsor Castle during his time as an Eton schoolboy in circumstances that to Orwell, remembering the event nearly thirty years later, seem extraordinarily dramatic: 'a sort of electric shock seemed to go through the street. People were taking their hats off, soldiers springing to attention. And then, clattering over the cobbles, came a huge, plum-coloured open carriage drawn by four horses with postilions.' But Orwell barely notices the queen. Instead his eyes are fixed on the groom lodged on the carriage's rear seat, immobile, dressed in white breeches and with a cockade on his top hat. Even in 1920, Orwell concludes, 'it gave me a wonderful feeling of looking backwards through a window into the nineteenth century'. Much of Orwell's work brings off this effect. On another occasion he recalls the inscriptions sometimes placed on Victorian graves in the sprawling municipal cemeteries of east London commemorating the deceased, his wife and 'two or three children of the above', so much time and so many childbirths having elapsed that no one could quite remember how many offspring the man had fathered. Like Queen Mary's carriage seen in Windsor high street, it is a perfect example of both Orwell's eye for history and the profound gap that separates a bygone age from our own.

◉

Orwell's view of the past was intimately bound up with his upbringing. Like the Reverend Hare, Richard Blair was of aristocratic descent, the great-grandson of an eighteenth-century Fane, earl of Westmorland. Since that time the family's fortunes had relied on the empire, slavery – Orwell's great-grandfather had owned a plantation in Jamaica – and government service. By the mid-Victorian era, on the other hand, the Blairs were in sharp decline. Orwell's father, the last of ten children, was a middle-ranking civil servant who never earned more than a few hundred pounds a year and on returning to England shortly before the Great War was forced to eke out his pension with the secretaryship of the local golf club. Much of the family's limited resources were concentrated on Eric, who was sent to a fashionable prep school (albeit at reduced fees), won a King's Scholarship to Eton College, the country's most prestigious public school, and of whom, at an early age, great things were expected. With the precision that he brought to nearly all forms of social hierarchy, Orwell defined his background as 'lower-upper-middle class'. By this he meant that most of the social expertise the Blairs were assumed to possess was theoretical rather than actual. They were, he once remarked, the kind of people who were supposed to keep servants, but in practice could never afford more than a solitary daily help.

The (relative) privilege of his early years meant that the social baggage Orwell had picked up in childhood could rarely be discarded as he grew older. Almost everyone who came across him in later life quickly identified him as a 'gentleman'. There was a particularly awkward moment out on the road researching *Down and Out in Paris and London* when the tramp major in a casual ward, seeing that Orwell had given his occupation as 'journalist', commiserated with him for having come down in the world: 'Well, that's bloody bad luck, governor. That's bloody bad luck, that is.' If Orwell was betrayed by his accent – irredeemably that of an ex-public schoolboy, friends maintained – then his social origins were also apparent in some of the figurative language that strays into his books (in *Keep the Aspidistra Flying*, the headgear worn by Gordon's girlfriend Rosemary is likened to 'a Harrow boy's hat') and in an unquestioning reverence for the protocols he had been brought up to respect. A visitor to the Inner Hebridean island of Jura, where he lived on and off in the late 1940s, remembered that when his landlord and fellow Old Etonian Robin Fletcher came to tea, he and Orwell took their meal in the sitting room while the other guests were confined to the kitchen.

To do him justice, Orwell was aware of his inconsistencies in this line. He knew that many of the working-class people with whom he came into contact in the course of his professional life had identified him as a toff and, in consequence, did not know how to treat him (the trade unionists and Labour Party members he encountered on the *Road to Wigan Pier* journey alternated between calling him 'Comrade' and 'Sir'). But he was also aware that he could not have jettisoned his profound attachment to the world in which he had been born without being false to the kind of person he imagined himself to be. As he wrote in 'Why I Write', 'I am not able, and I do not want, completely to abandon the views that I acquired in childhood.' Significantly, he then goes on to concede that with a fairer wind behind him the pull of the first three impulses he discerns behind the act of literary composition – egoism, aesthetic enthusiasm and historical purpose – would probably have outweighed ideological intent. 'In a peaceful age I might have written ornate or merely descriptive books, and might have remained almost unaware of my political loyalties. As it is I have been forced into being a sort of pamphleteer.'

All this had serious consequences for the persona he brought to both his professional and social life. What might be termed the class angle winds through *A Clergyman's Daughter* like knotweed through a lawn. You can tell within a few pages that the man who wrote it enjoyed a classical education and is thoroughly au fait with the work-ings of the Church of England at bedrock, parish level. The class angle, too, is a feature of Orwell's friendships. Although his acquaint-ance extended to almost every social level – he was as happy to lunch at the Ritz with Bertrand Russell as to wander the backstreets of Islington with the bohemian poet Paul Potts – a significant percentage of his friends came from a similar background to his own: upper-middle class, public school-educated, and from families with a long tradition of military or public service. Anthony Powell's father was a lieutenant-colonel; Malcolm Muggeridge's had been a Labour MP. There is almost certainly a social basis to Orwell's admiration for the writings of Evelyn Waugh (Waugh was a publisher's son from Hampstead and, like Orwell, descended from generations of Lowland Scots) and one of the most fascinating pieces Orwell ever wrote was an essay on Waugh's novels, begun sometime in mid-1949 and left unfinished at his death.

In the wake of *Brideshead Revisited*, published four years before, Orwell is quick to note Waugh's 'romantic belief in aristocracy'. But he insists that for all the 'high-spirited foolery' of his books, his essential scheme is serious: 'What Waugh is trying to do is to use the feverish, cultureless modern world as a set-off for his own conception of a good and stable way of life.' Significantly, the novel of Waugh's that seems most to absorb him is *Vile Bodies* (1930), a satirical account of the party-going, practical-joke-enamoured Bright Young Things who took up almost permanent residence in the gossip columns of the 1920s. And yet his real interest is reserved less for the Hon. Agatha Runcible, Miles Malpractice and the rest of Waugh's rackety cast than for a minor episode towards the end of the novel in which a collection of rather older guests assembles for a party at a great house in the West End:

> a great concourse of pious and honourable people (many of whom made the Anchorage House reception the one outing of the year), their women-folk well gowned in rich and durable stuffs, their men-folk ablaze with orders; people who had represented their country in foreign places and sent their sons to die for her in battle, people of decent and temperate life, uncultured, unaffected, unembarrassed, unassuming, unambitious people, of independent judgment and marked eccentricities, kind people who cared for animals and the deserving poor, brave and rather unreasonable people, that fine phalanx of the passing order, approaching, as one day at the Last Trump, they hoped to meet their Maker, with decorous and frank cordiality to shake Lady Anchorage by the hand at the top of her staircase . . .

As Orwell points out, this is not meant to be funny. Rather, it is an 'irrelevant outburst' intended to showcase the merits of people 'who still have, or used to have, a sense of obligation and a fixed code of behaviour, as against the mob of newspaper peers, financiers, politicians and playboys with whom the book deals'.

It can be seen from these remarks that Orwell identifies both with Lady Anchorage's guests, who, if they occupy a slightly higher rung on the social ladder, share the moral outlook of his parents' generation, and with Waugh's aim to provide a counterblast to the air of frivolity and short-term pleasure-seeking of which the novel mostly consists. Although the two men were worlds apart both politically and spiritually – Waugh was a right-wing Roman Catholic – there was clearly much more to bring them together than to drive them apart. Waugh was a fan of *Animal Farm*, sent Orwell a critique of *Nineteen Eighty-Four* and, after visiting him in the sanatorium in Gloucestershire a few months before he died, confided to their mutual friend Cyril Connolly that the patient was 'near to God'.

◎

God was as much a part of Orwell's upbringing as dreadnoughts in the Channel and history lessons about thin red lines and the charge of the Light Brigade at Balaclava. Like most upper-bourgeois children of his generation he was brought up according to the rites of the Church of England, was confirmed, when at Eton, by Charles Gore, the bishop of Oxford, and, while at prep school, Eton and serving in the Burma police force, would have attended hundreds of church services as a matter of routine. But for all his widely canvassed lack of religious belief, Orwell's attitude to the faith he was born into is not easy to decipher. On the one hand, he went through a definite spiritual 'phase' while living in west London in the early 1930s, which involved reviewing religious books, taking a serious interest in Roman Catholicism, attending the local church, making a friend of the curate and bragging to Suffolk friends about early-morning trips to Holy Communion. If nothing else, the early chapters of *A Clergyman's Daughter*, with their echoes of the doctrinal controversies of the interwar era, are hard evidence that when it came to the workings of the Anglican Church, Orwell knew what he was talking about. Clearly Orwell was interested in, and amused by, the paraphernalia of the church, its outlandish vestments and the bitter internecine warfare of its rival factions. But once one has stripped away the broad outline of Dorothy's adventures, in Suffolk and beyond, what remains is a novel about what, at the time of its publication, was a highly old-fashioned subject: religious doubt.

God's good grace, his infinite concern for meek humanity, his habit of manifesting himself at times of crisis, are to Dorothy something real and actual: at the novel's outset her belief in the existence of God is probably greater than her belief in the existence of Australia. There is a revealing scene in the very first chapter when, attending early-morning communion in her father's church, she struggles to pray, only to be reassured by a shaft of sunlight that suddenly irradiates a spray of leaves in the vestibule: 'It was as though some jewel of unimaginable splendour had flashed for an instant, filling the doorway with green light.' On the instant, Dorothy is consumed by joy. 'The flash of living colour had brought back to her, by a process deeper than reason, her peace of mind, her love of God, her power of worship.' Two hundred and fifty pages later, back in Knype Hill after nine months away and chastened by what has happened to her in the interim, she can only brood about 'the deadly emptiness that she had discovered at the heart of things'. What has happened to 'the well-meaning, ridiculous girl who had prayed ecstatically in summer-scented fields and pricked her arm as a punishment for sacrilegious thoughts'? The problem, Dorothy divines, is that she is still the same girl. 'Beliefs change, thoughts change, but there is some inner part of the soul that does not change.' Faith may vanish, 'but the need for faith remains the same as before'.

There follow several paragraphs of what can only be described as existential brooding. If no ultimate purpose redeems the detail of your life, Dorothy reflects, then existence takes on a quality of greyness 'which you could feel like a physical pang at your heart'. Surely only fools or self-deceivers can face that fact without flinching? Faith, to the disillusioned rector's daughter, is 'all or nothing. Either life on earth is a preparation for something greater and more lasting, or it is meaningless, dark and dreadful.' The fascination of this passage rests on the fact that Dorothy, who when the scene begins is hard at work devising costumes for a charity pageant, is reminded of her duties by the smell of the glue-pot bubbling on the stove. Instantly, she is returned to another part of her heritage – the glittering panoply of English history that constitutes the past ('After Julius Caesar there was William the Conqueror to be thought of. More armour!'). Significantly, the simple act of having to trudge to the scullery and refill the saucepan brings her back to earth. All across the world, she divines, there are millions of people in the same predicament: believers who have lost their faith without losing their need *of* faith. All one can do is deal as effectively as possible with the reality that lies nearby, accept that 'faith and no faith are very much the same provided that one is doing something that is customary, useful and acceptable'.

And so Dorothy goes on making costumes for the pageant, half of her thinking about God and half of her thinking about bygone English life ('After William the Conqueror – was it chain mail in William the Conqueror's day? – there were Robin Hood and a bow and arrow – and Thomas à Becket in his cope and mitres, and Queen Elizabeth's ruff . . .') without realising that the two are intimately connected. In the context of Orwell's later writings, all this is highly prophetic, for what lies at the heart of his critiques of totalitarianism is an awareness of the part played in them by displaced religious sensibility. The specimen autocrat of the mid-twentieth century denies the existence of God, and the refusal of a belief in divine judgment allows him to behave as he wants. Reviewing Malcolm

Muggeridge's book about the 1930s, for example, Orwell concedes that religious belief had to be abandoned once it became a tool of the governing classes, 'a semi-conscious device for preserving social and economic distinctions'. On the other hand, the materialism and 'progress' that have supplanted it have failed to meet that deep-seated need for faith. If one assumes that no sanctions are effective except the prospect of supernatural punishment, then 'it is clear what follows. There is no wisdom except the fear of God; but nobody fears God; therefore there is no wisdom.' The tyrant can do as he pleases and the future can look after itself.

To Orwell, the 'modern cult of power worship' is inextricably bound up with an acceptance that there is no life beyond the grave. A *Tribune* piece from 1944 echoes Dorothy's broodings over the glue-pot: there can be no worthwhile picture of the future, he declares, 'unless one realises how much we have lost by the decay of Christianity'. Comments of this sort are strewn throughout his work. At exactly the same time that Orwell was writing *A Clergyman's Daughter* in the early part of 1934 he filed a review of a book about the French poet Charles Baudelaire for the *Adelphi*. Here Orwell concludes – approvingly – that the subject 'clung to the ethical and the imaginative background of Christianity, because he had been brought up in the Christian tradition and because he perceived that such notions as sin, damnation etc., were in a sense truer and more real than anything he could get from sloppy humanitarian atheism'. This, too, is a prophetic passage. Orwell's attachment to the ethical and imaginative background of Christianity is one of the things that makes him distinctive as a writer, and the dilemmas that afflict Dorothy Hare as she sits manufacturing Julius Caesar's breastplate out of stiffened cardboard are very much his own.

◎

Inevitably, the scent of heritage hung over the young Eric Blair's initial choice of career and the four and a half years (late 1922 to mid-1927) he spent in the Burma police. But Orwell's stint as servant of the British Raj, responsible for upholding law and order in one of the remoter parts of the empire, is often misrepresented, found to harbour patterns that it did not possess at the time, and subject to large amounts of retrospective fixing. More than one critic, examining the spectacle of a nineteen-year-old boy being sent to the further reaches of the globe – travelling to Burma involved an 8,000-mile month-long trip aboard a steamship – has seen it as a kind of dreadful exile from home and hearth wished on Orwell by his exacting and imperially minded family. In much the same way, his return home has often been interpreted as a symbolic gesture made by a man who had seen through the imperial racket and was determined to make amends for his involvement in it.

Neither of these interpretations, it turns out, is wholly accurate. For a teenage boy of Orwell's background who had not exerted himself at school, a job in the East would have seemed a perfectly reasonable destiny. Richard Blair had spent nearly forty years in India; his mother's Limouzin family had been established in Burma since the middle of the nineteenth century: just to ram home this ancestral connection, Orwell asked on his application form to be posted either to the United Provinces of British India, where his father had worked, or to Burma, where both his grandmother and his aunt were currently living. Exile this was not. As for Orwell's attitude to Burma once he got there, no one remembered him as anything other than a highly conventional young man who seems to have made a positive virtue of his inconspicuousness. Unlike Flory, the hero of *Burmese Days*, whom the other members of Kyauktada's European Club regard as a 'bit of a Bolshie', what with his constant criticisms of the way in which Burma is run, he kept his opinions to himself. Neither was his return from Burma in 1927 a decisive act of rejection. He came home on a medical certificate, after contracting dengue fever, in the knowledge that he would in any case have been entitled to six months' leave at the end of the year. Even more revealing of Orwell's state of mind at this period in his life is that he brought back an engagement ring which he intended to present to a girl named Jacintha Buddicom, the daughter of a neighbouring family in Shiplake, near Henley, whom he had known since his teens. In the event, Jacintha turned him down, but what if she had said yes? The chances are that the two of them would have gone straight back to Burma.

If Orwell's attitude to Burma while he was stationed there is beyond reconstituting, then his mature view of the country in which he had spent his early twenties is set in stone. Nearly all his writings about the East are thoroughly anti-imperial, and one of his very first published articles – a piece for the French newspaper *Le Progrès Civique* – is entitled 'How a Nation is Exploited: The British Empire in Burma'. Each of the targets Orwell sets up is thoroughly demolished – the Burmese political system convicted of 'latent despotism', its economy ruined by the depredations of 'get-rich-quick' businessmen with no interest in contributing to the well-being of the country, its relationship with Britain characterised as that of 'slave and master'. The autobiographical sections of *The Road to Wigan Pier* (1937) are full of symbolical reimaginings designed to convey Orwell's distaste for the job he had to do: the American missionary who stands watching a sub-inspector bullying a suspect and remarks, 'I wouldn't care to have your job'; the night on a train with an anonymous civil servant spent 'damning the British Empire', after which in the light of dawn 'we parted as guiltily as any adulterous couple' – each of these individual fragments eventually came to shape the mosaic of Orwell's views about empire, and their predominating emotion is guilt. Orwell spent long years reproaching himself for the 'monstrous intrusion' he and people like him had committed in the East and for the collusive silence that prevented it from ever being brought out into the open. 'Every Anglo-Indian is haunted by a sense of guilt which he usually conceals as best he can, because there is no freedom of speech, and merely to be overheard making a seditious remark may damage his career.'

Burmese Days (1934), the most considerable statement of Orwell's views about the British Empire, may even have been begun on the boat home from Rangoon: certainly one of its early drafts is written on Government of Burma notepaper. Orwell later admitted that, although not published until seven years after he had left the colonial service, it was 'projected much earlier'. As for its connection to his experience of serving the Raj, he once told another old Burma hand, the novelist F. Tennyson Jesse, that 'I daresay it's unfair in some ways, and inaccurate in some of its details, but much of it is simply reporting of what I have seen'. This is not to say that Flory, its disillusioned hero, is a projection of Orwell himself, merely that Orwell is clearly using him as a focus for some of the events he had witnessed in Burma and the dissatisfaction that burned in him by the time, sometime early in 1933, that he settled down to work on the book in earnest.

Flory, it has to be said, is a very typical Orwell hero: ground down, careworn, jaundiced (almost literally, as his skin has turned yellow in the tropical heat), solitary and near-friendless, his parents long dead, his only relatives a couple of sisters in England with whom he has long since lost touch. To add to these drawbacks, his face is disfigured by a hideous birthmark, 'stretching in a ragged crescent down his left cheek, from the eye to the corner of the mouth'. But Flory is a marked man in more than the literal sense. Now in his mid-thirties and miserably employed in the timber trade, he has fetched up in the town of Kyauktada, transparently based on Katha, Orwell's final posting ('The population was about four thousand, including a couple of hundred Indians, a few score Chinese and seven Europeans'), where he devotes his leisure hours to reading, getting drunk at the local club and talking to Dr Veraswami, the town's Indian doctor, about the iniquities of British rule: in a revealing contradistinction, the doctor turns out to be a passionate supporter of imperialism; it is left to Flory to point out some of its drawbacks. But Flory's relationship with Veraswami will prove to be his undoing, for the doctor has made an enemy of U Po Kyin, a fabulously corrupt and conniving native magistrate whose reach extends to almost every corner of local society and for whose targets even the possession of a white skin is no defence.

When the novel begins, Flory's emotional life, such as it is, is focused on Ma Hla May, his nest-feathering Burmese mistress. But the arrival in Kyauktada of Elizabeth Lackersteen, an ingenuous and lately orphaned twenty-year-old come to stay with her aunt and uncle and clearly on the lookout for a husband, brings home to him the aimlessness of his existence. Captivated by Elizabeth's charms (her Eton-cropped 'yellow hair as short as a boy's', a slender, youthful hand 'with the mottled wrist of a schoolgirl') and convinced by a few polite remarks about 'simply adoring reading' that he has chanced on a highbrow, Flory resolves to smarten himself up and set off in pursuit. Their relationship proceeds in leaps and bounds, including a mutually embarrassing visit to the local bazaar and a much more successful (and erotically charged) leopard hunt in the jungle, only for Flory's hopes to be thrown into jeopardy when the snobbish Mrs Lackersteen discovers that the haughty young cavalryman recently despatched to the area in charge of a squad of military police is the son of a peer. Detached from Elizabeth's affections by the Hon. Lieutenant Verrall, Flory manages to redeem himself by performing heroically in an insurrectionist attack on the club, only for a devious manoeuvre on U Po Kyin's part to disgrace him in her eyes. There can be no forgiveness: 'Never, never! I wouldn't marry you if you were the last person on earth.' Crazed with shame and disappointment, Flory goes back to his bungalow and blows his brains out.

What are we to make of Flory? On the one hand, he is clearly a victim of circumstances, a decent man, we infer, cast into misery and loneliness by the career he pursues. The excuse given for his evading military service during the Great War and opting to stay in Burma is that 'the East had already corrupted him, and he did not want to exchange his whisky, his servants and his Burmese girls for the boredom of the parade ground and the strain of cruel marches'. Even at the age of twenty-seven he realises that 'His youth [is] finished', that the years of 'Eastern life, loneliness and intermittent drinking [have] set their mark on him'. On the other hand, he is also complicit, a cog in the imperial wheel, a component in the vast imperial machine that pillages Burma of its natural resources and refuses to allow its people to govern themselves. The same dualism hangs over the two great sketches inspired by Orwell's time in Burma – 'A Hanging', published in the *Adelphi* in 1931, and 'Shooting an Elephant', which appeared in John Lehmann's *Folios of New Writing* in 1936.

Neither of these essays is quite what it seems on the surface. 'A Hanging', for example, though presented as reportage, owes an obvious debt to Thackeray's 'Going to See a Man Hanged' (1840); although he described it as an 'autobiographical sketch', local press reports of the incident on which 'Shooting an Elephant' seems to be based don't mention Orwell's name. While it has never been conclusively established that Orwell saw a man hanged or shot an elephant – a debate which so infuriated his widow Sonia that she once told a friend, 'Of course he shot the fucking elephant' – there is a way in which their grounding in the circumstances of his own life scarcely matters, for each offers a neat little parable of imperialism's effect on some of the people caught up in its net. The reader sympathises with the police officer ordered by his superiors to shoot the elephant that has suffered a temporary attack of madness and trampled a man to death, for the situation he has fetched up in is one he is unable to control. Surrounded by crowds of Burmese for whom the killing is a source of entertainment, he realises that he has no option but to pull the trigger: not to do so will mean losing face before the natives. At the same time, he is a servant of the Raj and, by implication, an oppressor. It is the same as the Burmese criminal goes to his death on the scaffold. If it weren't for the autocracy that his chronicler serves, the man would probably live.

Writers can only tell the truth about imperialism, Orwell suggests in *The Road to Wigan Pier*, if they have seen it from the inside. To see it from the inside was immediately to sympathise with some of the lower-league servants of empire, especially if they included members of your own family. When in *Burmese Days* he laments the destinies of retired Anglo-Indian civil servants ('They lead unenviable lives; it is a poor bargain to spend thirty years, ill-paid, in an alien country, and then come home with a wrecked liver and a pine-apple backside from sitting in cane chairs, to settle down as the bore of some second-rate club'), it is difficult not to imagine that he was thinking of his father, Richard Blair, who went out to the East in his teens and returned from it in his mid-fifties. Some of Orwell's sharpest digs are reserved for well-meaning liberals who presume to criticise an institution of which they have no real understanding from the comfort of an armchair in a Home Counties drawing room, the pacifists of Kipling's poem 'Tommy' who make mock of 'uniforms that guard you while you sleep'. As a servant of the Raj himself, he seems to have veered between sympathising with the oppressed races in his charge and being thoroughly exasperated both by their own behaviour and by enlightened attempts to proselytise on their behalf. The left-leaning *Adelphi* annoyed him so much, he told his friend Jack Common, that he sometimes tacked a copy to the trunk of a tree and used it for target practice. Half of him was appalled – if only retrospectively – by his professional duties, but the other half, as he once conceded, would have liked nothing better than to plunge a bayonet into a Buddhist priest's guts.

Nowhere are Orwell's equivocations about empire more apparent than when he settles down to consider a particular imperial hero such as Rudyard Kipling. The significance of his essay 'Rudyard Kipling', published in *Horizon* early in 1942 and a response to T.S. Eliot's *A Choice of Kipling's Verse* (1941), lies not only in what Orwell has to say about Kipling's poems but also in his response to the wider political context in which the poet can be located. Significantly he makes no attempt to justify the subject's 'jingoism' or his 'brutality', while resolutely defending him against charges of 'Fascism' ('He was further from being one than the most humane or the most "progressive" person is able to be these days'). And then, as he considers Kipling's relationship to the nineteenth-century Anglo-Indian world in which he spent his early life – Orwell suggests that his identification with the gang of administrators, soldiers and engineers who created the Victorian Raj is not so complete as it seems – the pull of heritage tugs him back:

> The nineteenth-century Anglo-Indians, to name the least sympathetic of his idols, were at any rate people who did things. It may be that all they did was evil, but they changed the face of the earth (it is instructive to look at a map of Asia and compare the railway system of India with that of the surrounding countries), whereas they could have achieved nothing, could not have maintained themselves in power for a single week, if the normal Anglo-Indian outlook had been that of, say, E.M. Forster.

When it comes down to it, a Victorian surveyor with a theodolite and a pair of field-glasses bent on constructing a railway line across a patch of scrub will always excite Orwell's admiration, for he is a person who 'did things'. *Burmese Days*, too, contains an odd little episode in which Orwell – unusually for a novel with a more or less undeviating moral line – seems faintly conflicted about one of his minor characters. This is the Hon. Lieutenant Verrall, whom Flory first encounters early one morning on the road outside his bungalow. The young soldier is carefully described. 'He was a youth of about twenty-five,' Orwell tells us, 'lank but very straight, and manifestly a cavalry officer.' Orwell always pays close attention to his characters' faces: Verrall's, we learn, is one of those 'rabbit-like' examples 'common to English soldiers, with pale blue eyes and a little triangle of fore-teeth visible between the lips'. A rabbit, perhaps, but, as we are quickly assured, 'a tough and martial rabbit' who sits on his horse 'as if he were part of it' and is, additionally, 'offensively young and fit'. As for Verrall's get-up, he is 'elegant as a picture' in his white buckskin topi and gleaming polo boots.

At this stage in the proceedings Verrall has not even met Elizabeth, much less supplanted Flory in her affections, yet the older man, sensing his inadequacy, is made 'uncomfortable from the start' and immediately embarrasses himself by tumbling from one of Verrall's horses in a vain attempt at tent-pegging. Even before this humiliation he is aware that he has 'never in his life felt so *de trop*, or so old and shabby'. Verrall, it soon becomes clear, is thoroughly obnoxious, treats most of the people he comes across with undisguised contempt, is rude, surly, mistreats the club servants in a way that even the local racists find unacceptable and, apart from Surtees's hunting stories, has not read a book since he was at school. On the other hand, it is equally clear that a part of Flory and by implication Orwell has a sneaking admiration for him. Take, for example, this account of Verrall's spartan lifestyle which follows a few pages later:

> Of course, like all sons of rich families, he thought poverty disgusting and that poor people are poor because they prefer disgusting habits. But he despised soft living. Spending, or rather owing, fabulous sums on clothes, he yet lived almost as ascetically as a monk. He exercised himself ceaselessly and brutally, rationed his drink and his cigarettes, slept on a camp bed (in silk pyjamas) and bathed in cold water in the bitterest winter. Horsemanship and physical fitness were the only gods he knew. The stamp of hoofs on the maidan, the strong, poised feeling of his body, wedded centaur-like to the saddle, the polo-stick springy in his hand – these were his religion, the breath of his life.

In addition, we learn that Verrall bears a 'charmed life' with regard to army discipline and that 'women of nearly all kinds threw themselves at his head'. It may very well be that Orwell had met Verrall, or someone like him, in his travels around Burma, but by this point the portrait has ceased to ring true. Ask what exactly Verrall is doing in *Burmese Days* and the answer would seem to be that Orwell has created a character who has got slightly out of hand and turned into a version of what a part of Orwell himself would have liked to be: a tough, no-nonsense cavalryman, untroubled by any doubts about the value of the job he does and, as such, the epitome of the imperial spirit.

The mature, politicised, left-wing Orwell was a convinced anti-imperialist, and yet several of the arguments he brought into play in the political debates of the 1940s had their origin on the right. The Kipling essay notes that 'A humanitarian is always a hypocrite, and Kipling's understanding of this is perhaps the central secret of his power to create telling phrases.' All left-wing parties in highly indus-trialised countries are ultimately a sham, Orwell argues, for their inter-nationalist aims are incompatible with a standard of living based on the exploitation of subject races. The same point is made three years before in a review of Clarence Streit's *Union Now* – which originally appeared under the provocative title 'Not Counting N——rs' – where Orwell notes that no real reconstruction of the imperial order can take place without at least a temporary drop in living standards, 'which is another way of saying that the majority of left-wing politicians and publicists are people who earn their living by demanding something they don't genuinely want'. Significantly, when he finally joined a political party in 1938, it was the Independent Labour Party, which believed that any outbreak of hostilities in Europe would take the form of an 'Imperialist war'.

As for what Orwell thought of the Anglo-Indian community in which he had been raised, and, more important, that community's attitude to the East, sympathy for his immediate family would always be countered by a more general sarcasm. George Bowling's memories of his in-laws, the Vincents, in *Coming Up for Air* are very close to caricature: 'Do you know these Anglo-Indian families? It's almost impossible, when you get inside these people's houses, to remember that out in the street it's England and the twentieth century.' Or there is the scene in his friend Stevie Smith's novel *The Holiday* (1949) in which a character named 'Raji' – based on the Indian writer Mulk

Raj Anand – addresses a meeting on the topic of English novelists who write about India. The air is heavy with the scent of patronage; the chairwoman remembers people she has known and loved in India, her ayah, dog and washerwoman. The meeting is eventually brought to a close by 'a young violent English person' who insists that no equality between intellectual Indians and English people is possible in India while 'this evil thing' – that is, the British Empire – still exists. All the evidence suggests that such a meeting actually took place at the Royal Indian Society sometime in the early 1940s and that the 'young violent English person' was Orwell. For all its deep-rooted attraction and the central part it played in his imaginative life, heritage could only take him so far.

The youthful Eric playing croquet with his Oxfordshire neighbours Prosper and Guinever Buddicom.

2

MYTHS AND LEGENDS

'SUCH, SUCH WERE THE JOYS' • *NINETEEN EIGHTY-FOUR*

Anthony Powell's novel *Books Do Furnish a Room* (1971) contains an extended portrait of the literary man X. Trapnel, author of such fictitious works as *Camel Ride to the Tomb* and *Profiles in String*. Talented and voluble, but also rackety and self-absorbed, Trapnel is every publisher's worst nightmare. Powell's aim in assembling the various materials that go to make up the Trapnel legend is not so much to define the kind of person that the subject is, but to analyse the kind of person he imagines himself to be, to itemise the wide variety of faces he offers to the world and to arrive at a general conclusion:

> Aiming at many roles, he was always playing one or other of them for all he was worth. To do justice to their number requires – in the manner of Burton – an interminable catalogue of types. No brief definition is adequate. Trapnel wanted, among other things, to be a writer, a dandy, a lover, a comrade, an eccentric, a sage, a virtuoso, a good chap, a man of honour, a hard case, a spendthrift, an opportunist, a *raissoneur*; to be very rich, to be very poor, to

possess a thousand mistresses, to win the heart of one love to whom he was ever faithful, to be on the best of terms with all men, to avenge savagely the lightest affront, to live to a hundred full years and honour, to die young and unknown but recognised the following day as the most neglected genius of the age. Each of these ambitions had something to recommend it from one angle or the other, with the possible exception of being poor – the only aim Trapnel achieved with unqualified mastery ...

There are fascinating Orwell connections here. Trapnel, as Powell acknowledged, is a projection of the writer Julian Maclaren-Ross (1912–64), whom Orwell knew during his days as literary editor of *Tribune* and to whom he offered considerable encouragement: 'Orwell sent mine back, saying it almost won the prize', runs a note referring to one of the magazine's short-story competitions found among Maclaren-Ross's papers after his death. As well as knowing and encouraging the younger man, Orwell was also an influence on his work: Maclaren-Ross's novel *Of Love and Hunger* (1947) not only owes a recognisable debt to *Keep the Aspidistra Flying* but even contains a character named Comstock. Just to emphasise the connection between Powell, Maclaren-Ross and Orwell, *Books Do Furnish a Room* turns out to be set in the icy metropolitan winter of 1946–7 – the last occasion on which Orwell was at large in literary London – and contains accounts of parties and social events whose real-life equivalents he very probably attended.

Like Maclaren-Ross, Orwell was a creature – and a purveyor – of myth. Some of the mythological trappings that surround him were the posthumous creation of his admirers; equally, there were others that he was keen to propagate himself. But immediately there are problems of definition. When old friends such as Muggeridge and Heppenstall talk about the 'Orwell myth', what exactly do they mean? When Muggeridge writes of 'seeing the legend of a man being created', he is referring to the groundswell of emotion provoked by the circumstances of Orwell's death: the solitary Cold War warrior, alone on his Hebridean island, struggling to complete a prophetic masterpiece before death snatches him away. Naturally Orwell had nothing to with these imaginings, and such accounts as we have of his last days on Jura are resolutely downbeat. But there are other Orwell myths whose origins lie closer to home. How did Orwell see himself as a personality? If Trapnel–Maclaren-Ross's shape-shifting is well-nigh cosmic in its scope, then Orwell's personal quest seems to have focused on the narrower target of expertise. All the evidence suggests that he envisioned himself as a thoroughly practical man, a dog-fancier, a smallholder (much of his time in Hertfordshire and Scotland was spent growing crops and raising animals), a carpenter, a lathe operator, a manufacturer of furniture. In his memoirs Powell recalls a conversation from the mid-1940s when Orwell and Eileen were living in a north-west London maisonette: '"If I have a dog, I always think my dog is the best dog in the world," he used to say, "or if I make anything at carpentry, I always think it's the best shelf or bookcase. Don't you ever feel the need to do something with your hands? I even like rolling my own cigarettes. I've installed a lathe in the basement. I don't think I could exist without my lathe."'

It was the same with the natural world and the rural lore that accompanied it. Powell, again, remembered Orwell and Eileen visiting his family in Kent towards the end of the war. On country walks Orwell would point out 'almost with anxiety' shrubs that were budding early or rare specimens not often seen in the south of England and draw attention to variations in the latching of field gates. In the end, though, little of this pursuit of expertise amounted to very much. A friend whose timber-merchant father supplied Orwell with some lengths of cherry wood with which to fashion some bookshelves was appalled by the result. Heppenstall, visiting the Hertfordshire cottage and its smallholding in 1938, was unimpressed: 'There were two goats in a stinking shed at the back, and the Blairs rented a strip of ground, across the road at the front and above road-level, in which they grew vegetables.' As for Orwell the 'practical man', the notorious incident in which a party setting off by boat from Jura through the Corryvreckan whirlpool narrowly escaped drowning was a result of his having misread the tide tables.

Admittedly, these are superficial aspects of the image of himself that Orwell liked to offer to the world. Much more long-lasting – and much more important to his work – is the view that he took of his early life, and in particular his childhood. As an adult, Orwell seems to have gone out of his way to convey the impression that he had not been happy as a child, that he was lonely and comparatively friendless, and that these deprivations inspired him with the urge to write. As he puts it in 'Why I Write', 'I had the lonely child's habit of making up stories and holding conversations with imaginary persons, and I think from the very start my literary ambitions were mixed up with the feeling of being isolated and undervalued.' The 'private world' thereby created was important to him as it offered a medium in which 'I could get my own back for my failure in everyday life.' The exact circumstances of Orwell's childhood are beyond recall, but the idea that the young Eric Blair was lonely, undervalued and 'not altogether happy' was one that his family and close friends were determined to rebut. His sister Avril, for example, left some pointed remarks about 'it' – that is, the claims about isolation and undervaluing – not being 'in the least true', a denial given extra spice by Avril's further comment that the judgement was retrospective: 'he did give out that impression when he was grown-up.'

There is plenty of evidence to bear out the second statement: P.G. Wodehouse, who met Orwell once during the war, came away from their solitary encounter in occupied Paris with the distinct impression that Orwell suffered as a child. But those who were there at the time thought otherwise. Jacintha Buddicom's memoir paints a picture of a lively, high-spirited boy, not at all distressed by intimations of social inadequacy or the sense of having 'failed'. Certainly Orwell's childhood was dominated by his father's absence – Richard Blair retired from the Indian Civil Service in 1912 at the age of fifty-five – but his mother's letters to friends (and indeed Orwell's letters to her) suggest that her children ('my chicks') were showered with affection. In later life Orwell would come to believe that he had been her favourite child. Nonetheless, the tocsin of an unhappy childhood clangs on through his autobiographical writings, and never more so than in his efforts to memorialise the five years that he spent at St Cyprian's, the immensely fashionable south-coast preparatory school that he entered as a boy of eight and a quarter in the autumn of 1911 and left sixteen terms later at the age of thirteen and a half.

The formal record of Orwell's time at St Cyprian's – where his contemporaries included Cyril Connolly and the future photographer and set designer Cecil Beaton – is a riot of achievement. He won prizes, was regularly complimented by visiting examiners, gained a reputation as the school's most promising poet – Connolly attests to this – and in his last term succeeded in winning scholarships to both Eton and Wellington, two of England's leading public schools. It is not an exaggeration to say that at thirteen Orwell was one of the cleverest boys in the country, a teenage Admirable Crichton who, in ordinary circumstances, could have been expected to proceed to a dazzling career as an Oxford don, a King's Counsel or a colonial administrator. His letters home, though doubtless censored by the authorities, are highly conventional. There is no hint among the recitation of sports results and enquiries after pets that 'Eric' isn't enjoying himself. Jacintha, too, caught no trace of dissatisfaction. She remembered him joking about snobbish Mrs Wilkes, the wife of the school's headmaster ('To be a favourite with Old Mum you have to be a duke in a kilt'), but the remarks were made in a spirit of mild satire rather than to register the existence of a score that needed to be settled.

Orwell bade farewell to his prep school days shortly before Christmas 1916. There is no mention of St Cyprian's in his writings for the next twenty-two years. Then, in December 1938, he writes to Connolly from Morocco about his old friend's newly published

Enemies of Promise, in whose long autobiographical section the school features as 'St Wulfric's'. In a densely evocative paragraph, Orwell remembers their shared literary interests from a quarter of a century ago. 'Do you remember one or other of us getting hold of H.G. Wells's "Country of the Blind" about 1914, at St Cyprian's, and being so enthralled with it that we were constantly pinching it off each other?' Then, without warning, the tone of the letter shifts. 'And do you remember at about the same time my bringing back to school a copy of Compton Mackenzie's *Sinister Street*, which you began to read and then that filthy old sow Mrs Wilkes found out and there was a fearful row about bringing "a book of that kind" . . . into the school.' Orwell ends up by expressing a wish to follow where Connolly has led. 'I'm always meaning one of these days to write a book about St Cyprian's. I've always held that the public schools aren't so bad, but people are wrecked by those filthy private schools long before they get to public school age.'

Another eight and a half years of silence follows. Then, in April 1947, St Cyprian's turns up again, in the course of an update on the progress of *Nineteen Eighty-Four* sent to Orwell's publisher Fredric Warburg. Here, after assuring Warburg that he is 'pegging away' at the novel, Orwell adds that he is sending under separate cover 'a long autobiographical sketch', first undertaken as a 'pendant' to *Enemies of Promise*. This is the first mention of 'Such, Such Were the Joys', which would not be published until 1952, two years after Orwell's death, and even then only in America, such was the fear of a libel suit from Mr and Mrs Wilkes. What sort of a piece of writing is 'Such, Such Were the Joys' and how did it come to be written? All the evidence suggests that Orwell took pains with the essay, spent long hours writing and rewriting it and thought highly of the finished product. We know, for example, that it was retyped at least three times before the author was satisfied, and the fact that he mentions it to Warburg in the same breath as *Nineteen Eighty-Four* suggests that at this point in his career it shared equal billing in his imagination.

But 'Such, Such Were the Joys' is an odd piece of work altogether. Over 15,000 words long, remorseless and self-pitying, its autobiographical positioning is stealthily undercut by literary influences. There are clear links to Thackeray's early work, to the school scenes in *David Copperfield* (1850) and to Samuel Butler's *The Way of All Flesh* (1903). Orwell himself once suggested that the view he took of the world was inspired by his early exposure to Dickens: 'I must have been about nine years old when I first read *David Copperfield*,' he remembered, adding that 'The mental atmosphere of the opening chapters was so immediately intelligible to me that I vaguely imagined they had been written *by a child*.' At the same time, any thought that Orwell might, albeit subconsciously, be paying tribute to some of the books that had beguiled his adolescence is altogether eclipsed by the bitterness of the tone. The essay begins with an epic description of the torments Orwell suffers at St Cyprian's for the crime of repeatedly wetting his bed. After a dressing-down at the hands of Mrs Wilkes, made worse by the presence of a disdainful lady visitor, Orwell is eventually taken off to be caned by her husband with a riding crop. Having made the mistake of being overheard telling another boy that the beating hasn't hurt, he is then marched back into the headmaster's study for a second assault so vicious that the riding crop breaks apart. The mature Orwell's account of this episode tries to analyse the various psychological impulses at work:

I had fallen into a chair, weakly snivelling. I remember that this was the only time throughout my boyhood when a beating actually reduced me to tears, and curiously enough I was not even now crying because of the pain. The second beating had not hurt very much either. Fright and shame seemed to have anaesthetised me. I was crying partly because I felt that this was expected of me, partly from genuine repentance, but partly also because of a deeper grief which is peculiar to childhood: a sense of desolate loneliness and helplessness, of being locked up not only in a hostile world but in a world of good and evil where the rules were such that it was not actually possible to keep them.

To the eight-year-old boy, the beating is a 'turning-point', a kind of climacteric that enables him to grasp a vital truth about the way the world works. He is miserably becalmed 'in a world where it is *impossible* for me to be good'. He is punished for a bodily function over which he has no control: above this misdemeanour looms the vision of a world whose proscriptions are that much worse for being arbitrary. Orwell represents his younger self as becoming aware for the first time in his life of the 'harshness' of the environment in which he has been set down. 'I had a conviction of sin and folly and weakness which I do not remember to have felt before.' Like Winston Smith, he is not only doomed but also unable to do anything to rescue his position. However well he may attempt to behave, whatever deals he may try to strike with vigilant authority, the rules will always shift against him.

Having established his own helplessness in the face of vigilant authority, Orwell goes on to convict the Wilkeses – invariably referred to by their nicknames of 'Sambo' and 'Flip' – of callousness, snobbery and favouritism. The rich boys have milk and biscuits in the middle of the morning, are addressed by their Christian names – in the case of aristocratic boys occasionally by their titles – and, most important of all, are never caned. Orwell, on the other hand, allowed into this intellectual forcing house for the sons of the well-to-do at reduced fees on the grounds that he was likely to enhance the school's reputation by winning a public-school scholarship, is constantly having the fact thrown in his face. Treats, cricket bats and other paraphernalia are denied him on the grounds that 'Your parents wouldn't be able to afford it', and several anguished sentences are devoted to the St Cyprian's tradition of supplying a boy with an iced cake on his birthday. This would be shared out at tea, with the cost charged up to his parents' account. 'I never had such a cake. Year after year, never daring to ask, I would miserably hope that this year a cake would appear.'

There are further complaints about the food, remembered as not only bad but insufficient: 'Never before or since have I seen butter or jam spread on bread so thinly.' At one point Orwell represents himself as stealing downstairs in the small hours to pilfer stale bread from the pantry. But these deprivations are not simply physical. As 'Such, Such Were the Joys' grinds inexorably on, it soon becomes clear that the main impact on Orwell, and by implication on his fellow-pupils, is psychological. Mrs Wilkes is emotionally capricious, extending her favours one day and withdrawing them the next, alternating benign approval and sorrowful injunctions to buck up. The result is that her young charges never really know where they stand and live in constant fear of failing to live up to her high but apparently arbitrary standards. Worse even than this is the atmosphere of continual surveillance. One of the most striking passages involves Orwell making an illicit visit to a sweetshop. As he leaves he notices a 'small, sharp-faced man who seemed to be staring very hard at my school cap'. Divining that the man is a spy, placed there by the headmaster, Orwell spends the next few days waiting for a summons to Mr Wilkes's study and is astonished when it fails to materialise. 'It did not seem to me strange that the headmaster of a private school should dispose of an army of informers, and I did not imagine that he would even have to pay them.'

And yet in some ways none of this is quite as unsettling as the finale. Orwell left St Cyprian's in a blaze of academic glory. He had won a scholarship to Wellington, with a second award in prospect at Eton once a place fell vacant (in the event he spent a solitary term at Wellington before changing schools in the summer of 1917) and could be regarded as one of the Wilkeses' prize pupils whose achievements could be used as bait for new recruits. But this is not how the mature Orwell saw it. In his retelling, Mrs Wilkes's parting smile is horribly ambiguous. 'You haven't made much of a success of your time at St Cyprian's, have you?' Orwell judges her to be implying. 'And I don't suppose you'll get on awfully well at a public school either. We made a mistake, really, in wasting our time and money on you.' Even more disquieting is Orwell's sense that the Wilkeses have found him out, discovered aspects of his character and beliefs that he hoped he had managed to keep hidden. Thus, Sambo and Flip 'know all about those ideas you have in the back of your head', they know he disbelieves everything he has been taught, that he isn't 'in the least grateful for all we've done' for him. Another boy might have been quietly satisfied at this inferred reaction. Orwell, however, is oppressed by a feeling of guilt. 'Failure, failure, failure – failure behind me, failure ahead of me – that was by far the deepest conviction I carried away.'

◉

Orwell took a lively interest in underachievement. All human life was a succession of failures, he once declared, and only the very young or the very foolish thought different. Did the events outlined in 'Such, Such Were the Joys' really happen? Or is Orwell reworking and embroidering his memories of childhood in a way that suits the view he took of himself as an adult? The final paragraphs, in particular, strike an oddly unconvincing note, for the psychology has clearly been tacked on afterwards, given a retrospective gloss by an adult sensibility that has spent long, embittered years brooding about times past. And how can a thirteen-year-old leaving school in a blaze of academic glory consider himself a 'failure'? In some ways, these distinctions scarcely matter: a century and more after they took place, the humiliations inflicted on the young Eric Blair by the Wilkeses – if they really were humiliations – are less important than the things they inspired. As for the authenticity of his attacks on Sambo and Flip, most of his St Cyprian's contemporaries and almost all of the writers who left accounts of their prep school days in the early years of the twentieth century are convinced that he was exaggerating. Certainly, conditions were spartan – Orwell's complaints about the poor food should be seen in the context of Great War-era rationing, and discipline was rigorously enforced: even Evelyn Waugh's brother Alec, who remembered his own school with the greatest enthusiasm, admitted that he was once forced to eat the contents of a porridge bowl into which he had recently vomited. Certainly, St Cyprian's had an unusual atmosphere: Connolly – another victim of Mrs Wilkes's capriciousness – talks about its 'voodoo' quality, but no one other than Orwell remembered Mr Wilkes as a flogger or recalled bright boys taken in on half-fees – standard practice in the scholarship-hungry prep schools of the time – having attention drawn to their parents' lack of means. There were old boys who disliked Mrs Wilkes and taught their children to shake their fists at the school when they passed it in a car, but there was no other case of a former pupil who imagined that their infant lives had been systematically warped by Sambo, Flip and the deference extended to those boys whose parents' income exceeded £2,000 a year.

What to make of all this? The really intriguing aspect of 'Such, Such Were the Joys' is the date of its composition. And when was this exactly? Theoretically, it could have been written at any date between early 1939, shortly after the letter to Connolly about *Enemies of Promise*, and some time in 1946. Mrs Miranda Christen, who did secretarial work for Orwell in the immediate post-war era, remembered that the version she sat down to retype had a battered air, denoting a fair amount of circulation. None of Orwell's friends seems to have heard any mention of it. The probability is that an existing version, whose roots extended deep into the early 1940s (but this is only a speculation), was coaxed into its final shape during Orwell's first extended stay on Jura, in other words at exactly the same time that he set seriously to work on *Nineteen Eighty-Four*. If the chronological relationship between essay and novel is impossible to disentangle, then the emotional atmosphere that pervades the two is surprisingly consistent. It is not simply that St Cyprian's is occasionally made to resemble a police state, what with the little men on street corners who are Sambo's spies and the constant feeling that one is being spied upon, but that the technique works in reverse. In fact, the world of O'Brien, interrogation and the Ministry of Love can often look like a private school of the St Cyprian's type.

One sees this immediately in the scenes in which O'Brien harangues Winston over the question of his 'defective memory' as a prelude to encouraging him not merely to pretend that two and two make five but actively to believe it. At one point, here in a torture chamber, with a dial ready to send electrical charges whistling through Winston's synapses, O'Brien's manner becomes oddly conciliatory, or at any rate 'less severe': 'He resettled his spectacles thoughtfully, and took a pace or two up and down. When he spoke his voice was gentle and patient. He had the air of a doctor, a teacher, even a priest, anxious to explain and persuade rather than to punish.'

It is the same a couple of pages later, when O'Brien raises the spectre of 'doublethink' by attempting to convince Winston that a photograph he has just destroyed never existed in the first place. Here he is described as looking down 'speculatively' on the figure strapped to the chair. More than ever 'he had the air of a teacher taking pains with a wayward but promising child'. All this raises the question of the victim's relationship with his tormentor. One of the most revealing passages in 'Such, Such Were the Joys' takes in Orwell's efforts to establish exactly what he thought of Flip. Naturally, he is keen to stay in 'favour': 'Whenever one had the chance to suck up, one did suck up, and at the first smile one's hatred turned into a kind of cringing love.' Such is the mesmerising power of Mrs Wilkes's personality that in her presence he is 'as helpless as a snake before the snake-charmer', and the shame inspired by being on the receiving end of one of her reproaches is enough to bring him to the brink of tears. For all the occasional attempts to achieve a sense of balance – Orwell remarks at one point that 'No one can look back on his schooldays and say with truth that he was always unhappy', and he has fond memories of going on butterfly hunts with a teacher named Brown – at the core of his being there lurks 'an incorruptible inner self' who knows that whatever he does 'one's only true feeling was hatred'.

This, too, has an echo in O'Brien's dealings with Winston. A part of him knows that O'Brien is trying to persuade him to deny the reality of his existence, but another part is anxious to please him, 'comforted' by the heavy arm placed round his shoulders when the torture stops: 'He had the feeling that O'Brien was his protector, that the pain was something that came from outside, from some other source, and that it was O'Brien who would save him from it.' At a later stage in the interrogation he is 'grateful' to his tormentor, 'and not merely because he had stopped the pain'. O'Brien, curiously, has become 'a person who could be talked to'; there exists somewhere 'a place where they could meet and talk'. Dominating their conversation, though, is Winston's feeling that it is impossible for him ever to meet the high standards expected of him. Just as the young Eric Blair could never attain the satisfaction of being permanently 'in favour' with Flip, so Winston can never quite work out what it is that O'Brien wants from him, or bring himself to believe in it once its dimensions take shape before him. Both of them are promising if slightly wayward pupils, worth taking pains with, sufficiently intelligent to have tricky concepts explained to them, to whom punishment is meted out more in sorrow than in anger.

There is no way of separating out the cross-currents of influence that connect 'Such, Such Were the Joys' and *Nineteen Eighty-Four*. It is perfectly possible that Orwell settled his scores with St Cyprian's some time before he went to work on the novel, while retaining some of the atmospherics of the earlier work. Equally, there is at least a chance that his preparations for the novel in 1945–6 gave him a psychological framework in which he could address his dealings with the Wilkeses. Given that Orwell first mentions the essay in a letter updating his publisher on the progress of the novel, the likelihood is that there was a brief period in which he worked at both projects simultaneously, and that the mental atmosphere transferred back and forth. St Cyprian's is like a police state; the nightmare world of Oceania, with its constant surveillance and its sneaking children, is like a school. Each denies the individual their autonomy and their private space; each substitutes an unquestioned autocratic code for self-determination. In writing 'Such, Such Were the Joys', Orwell is clearly drawing on psychological material that would not have been available to him as a child. Equally, *Nineteen Eighty-Four* sometimes seems to be referring us back to the schoolroom: that lost but terrifying space in which the real Orwell myth begins to flourish.

Burma police training school, Mandalay, 1923. Orwell stands third from the left.

3

GOING NATIVE

From the outset, Orwell seems always to have known that he would end up writing books for a living. 'Why I Write' begins with the admission that 'from a very early age, perhaps the age of five or six, I knew that when I grew up I should be a writer'. His earliest 'literary' memory was of dictating a poem to his mother about a William Blake-derived tiger with 'chair-like teeth'. A fair amount of juvenilia survives – patriotic poems that appeared in local newspapers, verses addressed to his teenage sweetheart Jacintha Buddicom, Etonian squibs – together with several hints that the ambition was seriously meant. Jacintha remembered many a conversation about that bright, romanticised future in which 'Eric' would feature as a 'FAMOUS AUTHOR' and recalled that the discussions got as far as the choice of a suitable binding for the collected edition. In late adolescence the dream seems to have been shoved aside by an awareness of some of the practical realities of middle-class life – Orwell notes that 'between the ages of about seventeen and twenty-four I tried to abandon this idea', while acknowledging that he 'did so with the consciousness that I was outraging my true nature' – and yet, within a week or two of returning to England in the summer of 1927, he had informed his parents not only that he intended to resign from the Burma police, but also that his sights were set on a career in literature.

In the context of Blair family life – its long tradition of imperial service, its resolute anti-intellectualism, all that dullness and philistinism Orwell commends in his remarks about Rosamond Lehmann's 'The Red-Haired Miss Daintreys' (p. 17) – this was an extraordinary change of tack. Richard and Ida Blair were outraged, and Orwell's father is supposed to have complained that his son was behaving like a 'dilettante', that is, a trifler who intended to dabble in a profession without any clear idea of what it might entail. Mr Blair, it should straightaway be said, had a point. It was not merely that Orwell was abandoning what was effectively a job for life, with a government pension awaiting him at its end, but that his immediate prospects were so precarious. Plenty of his contemporaries – some of them boys he had known, or known about, at school – were beginning to forge a career in the world of books: Evelyn Waugh would publish his first novel in 1928; Cyril Connolly had been taken up by the *New Statesman*; Harold Acton had already brought out two collections of poems. At the same time, most of the young men trying to make a name for themselves in the literary world of the late 1920s had advantages that Orwell himself sadly lacked: Waugh's father ran a publishing company and his brother Alec was a well-known novelist; Connolly had made a friend of the influential Bloomsbury critic Desmond MacCarthy; Graham Greene had a job on *The Times*. Wherever they turned, well-placed friends and sponsors were on hand to offer counsel. It is a mark of Orwell's inexperience that the person to whom he applied for advice in the autumn of 1927 was his one-time Eton tutor A.S.F. Gow, now a fellow of Trinity College, Cambridge, an eminent classical scholar and a shrewd judge of the written word, but no kind of guide to the living of the literary life here in interwar-era England.

Not much survives of the background to Orwell's early attempts to 'write', and what there is gives an impression of dogged, effortful

58

laboriousness. His friend Dennis Collings remembered him establishing himself in an upstairs room at his parents' house in Southwold with a pen and a heap of foolscap, not caring what he wrote but simply wanting to put words on paper. The poet Ruth Pitter, a family friend re-encountered when he moved to London, recalled of some of these early efforts: 'Like a cow with a musket'. The path to publication was slow: his first published article, 'La Censure en Angleterre', appeared in the French literary journal *Monde* in October 1928, to be followed, two months later, by 'A Farthing Newspaper' in *G.K.'s Weekly*. Again, the contrast with leading contemporary talents was painful. Waugh's *Decline and Fall* had made him a celebrity at the age of twenty-four; Connolly was a rising young critic with a foot in half a dozen Bloomsbury drawing rooms; but Orwell made his domestic debut in a small-circulation weekly magazine, run on a shoestring, that barely paid its contributors.

What drove him to write? Orwell's motivation in 1927 is not easy to decipher. Among the items he had brought back from Burma – these included several steamer trunks and a collection of tropical hats at which small children exclaimed when he wore them in the street – was an outsize helping of guilt. In the polemical second half of *The Road to Wigan Pier* (1937), Orwell offers a long and well-nigh agonised account of the way in which his feelings for the native Burmese whom he had spent four and a half years oppressing transferred themselves to the British working classes. It was the first time, he tells us, that he had ever been really aware of the working class, and to begin with his interest stemmed from the fact that they supplied an 'analogy':

> They were the symbolic victims of injustice, playing the same part in England as the Burmese played in Burma. In Burma the issue had been quite simple. The whites were up and the blacks were down, and therefore as a matter of course one's sympathy was with the blacks. I now realised that there was no need to go as far

as Burma to find tyranny and exploitation. Here in England, down under one's feet, were the submerged working class, suffering miseries which in their different way were as bad as any an Oriental ever knows.

Having established this link, Orwell goes on to make a distinction that would inform most of the fiction he wrote in the 1930s: that there are degrees of deprivation and that the shabby-genteel poverty of the hitherto 'respectable' working man is always the worst. Here in the late 1920s this knowledge had yet to be acquired: as Orwell admits, when he thought of poverty he thought of 'brute starvation'. His aim, consequently, was focused on 'the lowest of the low' – tramps, beggars, criminals, prostitutes: 'these were the people with whom I wanted to get in touch. What I profoundly wanted, at that time, was to find some way of getting out of the respectable world altogether.' If this target would, in the end, prove unrealisable, then 'at least I could go among these people, see what their lives were like and feel myself temporarily part of their world'. Once he had taken this step, 'part of my guilt would drop from me'.

However fervent this *apologia pro vita sua*, it is worth making the point that Orwell's explanation of the impulses that drove him to pick up his pen is retrospective, written nine years after he returned from the East and at a time when some of the political implications of the work he was bent upon were only just beginning to occur to him: looking back, the mature Orwell was recasting his life along lines that would probably have seemed a great deal less exact to his twenty-something avatar. And then, too, there is the backdrop of the literary world in which he had fetched up. Here in the aftermath of the Great War, the 1920s was an age in which all sorts of writers consciously set about rediscovering the England into which they had been born. It was an age of rural rides, of country rambles, of Chesterton's rolling English drunkard and his rolling English road. Some of this rediscovery was conspicuously up-market – one thinks of H.V. Morton's genre-defining *In Search of England* (1927) or the Georgian poets companionably at large in their Sussex back lanes – but there existed alongside it a strain of lowlife reportage that went back to Jack London's *People of the Abyss* (1903) and W.H. Davies's *Autobiography of a Super-tramp* (1908), and in some cases several decades beyond them. Orwell was a fan of Davies – he reviewed his *Collected Poems* for the *Observer* in 1943 – and admired, or would shortly come to admire, the novels of George Gissing, whose *Thyrza* (1887) and *The Nether World* (1889) are both set in working-class London and whose plots hang on the interactions and clashes between contending social classes.

From a very early stage in his life beyond the margins of 'respectable' English society, Orwell identified with the working classes. After Orwell's death, the *Observer*'s editor David Astor once asked his sister Avril whom her brother most admired. Astor expected her to name some writer or public figure, but Avril instantly shot back: 'The working-class mother of eight children.' His feeling for the miners whose working practices he scrutinised in the journey spent researching *The Road to Wigan Pier* is practically idolatrous. The diary of his hop-picking adventures in Kent in the summer of 1931, too, is full of compliments to friendly fellow labourers: 'There was one couple, a coster and his wife, who were like a father and mother to us. They were the kind of people who are generally drunk on Saturday nights and who tack a "fucking" on to every noun, yet I have never seen anything that exceeded their kindness and delicacy.' And yet most of Orwell's attempts to 'connect' with socio-economic categories beneath his own were doomed to failure. However much the people he met in the course of his travels responded to him or appreciated his efforts on their behalf, the class divide between them was usually too wide to breach.

There was a comic side to these attempts at solidarity. The novelist Peter Vansittart remembered being taken by Orwell to a pub in Fleet Street in the early 1940s and being lectured by him about his general appearance. 'The fact is that with a tie like that and an accent like that, you will never be accepted by the working classes as one of themselves.' Vansittart, an ex-public schoolboy and Oxford graduate, had no ambitions to be accepted by the working classes as 'one of themselves', but Orwell would not be gainsaid. Their conversation was interrupted by the pub landlord, who, enquiring if the 'gentlemen' would like another drink, addressed Vansittart as 'Peter' and Orwell as 'Sir'. It was the same with the Spanish Civil War veteran Jack Branthwaite who, invited to stay at the very modest Hertfordshire cottage Orwell and his first wife Eileen inhabited in the late 1930s, discovered that guests were encouraged to dress for dinner. Vansittart recalled the relish with which Orwell, on one of his pub excursions, would order up 'a pint', as if the usage alone would transport him through the otherwise impermeable membrane of class, and there is a rather revealing scene in *Keep the Aspidistra Flying* in which Gordon's wealthy patron Ravelston, taken to an establishment too poor to afford a spirits licence, betrays himself by ordering two double whiskies.

Orwell's apprenticeship, the period in his life when as the critic V.S. Pritchett put it, he 'went native in his own country', lasted from the autumn of 1927 to the moment in mid-1932 when the manuscript of *Down and Out in Paris and London* was accepted for publication by the firm of Victor Gollancz. Chronologically it takes in his initial tramping forays around London and the south-east, a twenty-month stint in Paris (1928–9) and a longer stretch of time, much of it beyond the biographer's grasp, in which he combined his researches with tutoring jobs in the Southwold area. As well as *Down and Out*, its souvenirs include 'The Spike', its material dating from the pre-Paris days but not published until 1931, 'Hop-Picking' (October 1931), the unpublished 'Clink', an account of Orwell's being arrested for drunkenness and spending the night in a police cell, and the terrific early poem 'A Dressed Man and a Naked Man', not published until the autumn of 1933 but drawing on his memories of the

London dosshouses and reimagining an encounter glanced at in *Down and Out*. Much of this experience was put to good use in Orwell's later work: his time spent in a Parisian hospital in the spring of 1929 is the basis of his 1946 essay 'How the Poor Die', while some of the remorseless detail on display in 'Clink' feeds into Gordon's incarceration in *Keep the Aspidistra Flying* and Winston Smith's time at the Ministry of Love in *Nineteen Eighty-Four*.

What kind of writer did Orwell want to be, here in the foothills of a career that would take many years properly to establish itself? The obvious answer is: a very old-fashioned one. This was the age of modernism, when such new-fangled techniques as stream-of-consciousness narration and cinematic dialogue were making their presence felt in the literary mainstream: Evelyn Waugh and Anthony Powell's early work is heavily indebted to the dandy-modernist Ronald Firbank (1886–1926), a writer of such exquisite obscurity that the average bookstall-browser or Boots Library-subscriber of the early 1930s would scarcely have heard mention of his name. Orwell was not immune to modernism's attractions – he was fixated on Joyce's *Ulysses* (see the Trafalgar Square scenes of *A Clergyman's Daughter*) – but the real influence on his novels came from the naturalist writers of twenty or thirty years before. *Burmese Days*, for example, owes a mighty debt to Conrad and Somerset Maugham. Orwell's admiration for Wells runs through his early work like the lettering through a stick of rock, and asked to take sides in the argument that produced Virginia Woolf's polemical attack on the realistic narratives of Arnold Bennett, 'Mr Bennett and Mrs Brown' (1924), he would almost certainly have plumped for the author of *Riceyman Steps*.

'Why I Write' makes no bones about these early affiliations. It is clear, Orwell decides, what kind of aesthetic path he wanted to follow: 'I wanted to write enormous naturalistic novels with unhappy endings, full of detailed descriptions and arresting similes, and also full of purple passages in which words were used partly for the sake of their sound. And in fact my first complete novel, *Burmese Days* . . . is rather that kind of book.' *Burmese Days'* other distinctive feature is its sheer over-excitement with scene, Orwell's aesthetic instincts being so stimulated by the locale in which he has been set down that what starts out as a backdrop soon begins to take centre-stage. As he once put it, 'In novels about the East the scenery is the real subject matter.' Take, for example, the second chapter's description of Flory leaving his bungalow for a visit to the Kyauktada Club. Beyond the latter the Irrawaddy River flows 'huge and ochreous, glittering like diamonds in the patches that caught the sun'. In the distance in the native town the spire of the pagoda rises from the trees 'like a slender spear tipped with gold'. It is the same when Flory approaches the club. Here he passes a shrubbery of native trees and bushes: 'gold mohur trees like vast umbrellas of blood-red bloom, frangipanis with creamy, stalkless flowers, purple bougainvillea, scarlet hibiscus and the pink Chinese rose'. A native servant with a watering can can be seen moving in the jungle of flowers 'like some large, nectar-sucking bird'.

A similar outpouring of aesthetic intent accompanies Flory and Elizabeth's trip to the bazaar, where the clothes worn by the mob of people milling are so multicoloured that the effect is 'like a cascade of hundreds-and-thousands poured out of a jar', and pomelo fruit dangle on strings 'like green moons'. Back at the Lackersteens' gate can be found a clump of hollyhocks eight feet high 'with round red flowers like blowsy girls' faces'. Significantly, it took Orwell several years to root out this impressionist, painterly side from his writing. *A Clergyman's Daughter* finds an elderly parishioner named Miss Mayfill at early morning communion 'doubling herself up like a geometrid caterpillar, with many creakings, and crossing herself so elaborately that one might have imagined that she was sketching a series of braid frogs on the front of her coat'. Even as late as *Keep the Aspidistra Flying*, Gordon, while wandering through a late-night street market, watches three girls bending over one of the stalls. The Lackersteens' hollyhocks are said to resemble girls' faces, but here

Orwell reverses the trick and makes the girls resemble flowers – 'three youthful faces, flower-like in the harsh light, clustering side by side like a truss of blossom on a Sweet William or phlox'. The desire to conflate natural and female beauty never left him; the few lyrical flourishes in *Nineteen Eighty-Four* tend to occur when Winston and Julia are out in the countryside and the noise of a thrush becomes 'a kind of liquid stuff that poured all over him and got mixed up with the sunlight that filtered through the leaves'.

But Orwell's real talent in these early days is for reportage: punctilious accumulations of detail, painstaking observations of crowded interiors and the people at large in them. 'A Dressed Man and a Naked Man' is not so much a poem as a description:

A dressed man and a naked man
Stood by the kip-house fire,
Watching the sooty cooking-pots
That bubble on the wire.
And bidding tanners up and down,
Bargaining for a deal,
Naked skin for empty skin,
Clothes against a meal.

At the same time, this ability to recapitulate his experiences and the research that accompanied them is not confined to the habits of tramps or the way in which the employees of an up-market Parisian hotel comport themselves below stairs. All of Orwell's 1930s novels contain passages which are concerned simply with unloading information which he has picked up somewhere along the way. Thus 'Hop-Picking', originally a *New Statesman* article, is transferred wholesale into *A Clergyman's Daughter*, while the accounts of Dorothy's experiences teaching in a west London private school read as if they come from another *New Statesman* article that had yet to be written. Similarly, the scenes set in Mr McKechnie's bookshop in

Keep the Aspidistra Flying are given a more personal gloss in 'Bookshop Memories', an evocative piece of reminiscence filed for the *Fortnightly Review* a few months after the novel itself was published. There is more book-world sociology on display in the chapter in which Gordon, now thoroughly on his uppers, fetches up in the twopenny library in Lambeth working for the rapacious Mr Cheeseman. A glance at the relevant trade directory confirms that no such establishment ever existed, but Orwell has clearly done his homework, knows how the business works and the kind of light reading it offers, and there is a definite relish about the manner in which he sets about transforming his raw materials into fiction.

Orwell's enthusiasm for sheer detail works in two ways. On the one hand, his patient descriptions and his verifiable facts – Dorothy and the village schoolmaster Victor Stone trading lines from *Hymns Ancient and Modern*, say – give his work a terrific tang of authenticity and reinforce its determinedly naturalistic air. Just as the reader of Zola's *L'Assommoir* (1877) knows that its author has spent time in a Parisian drinking den amid a cloud of absinthe fumes, so the reader of *A Clergyman's Daughter* can be certain that its author once taught in a seedy private school, where the government inspector never calls. Equally, there are times when the detail threatens to swamp the characters who foreground it, when the backdrop to the tapestry seems more important than the figures picked out in coloured thread. Meanwhile, there are other influences at work in Orwell's work whose existence suggests that his methods of converting what he witnessed or experienced into print were sometimes more complicated, if not devious, than they seem at first glance.

To begin with, there is Orwell's reliance on literary models – 'A Hanging', with its ghostly invocation of Thackeray's 'Going to See a Man Hanged', or 'How the Poor Die', which, as it acknowledges, was inspired not only by a memory of his treatment at the Hôpital Cochin but also by childhood exposure to Tennyson's 'In the Children's Hospital'. *The Road to Wigan Pier* offers a vivid account of Orwell's first foray into a down-and-out's hostel: the newcomer's nervous terror, the threat of violence, the drunken stevedore finally collapsing on his neck with a cry of "'Ave a cup of tea, chum' (Orwell notes of the cup of tea that 'It was a kind of baptism'). No one could doubt that it happened as Orwell says it happened, and yet the opening stretch of Davies's *Autobiography of a Super-tramp* pans out in almost exactly the same way. This is not to accuse Orwell of plagiarism, merely to point out that some of his early writing has a kind of extra-literary sheen, brought about by his habit of referring back to bygone great works.

These hybridising tendencies are a feature of *Down and Out in Paris and London* – less so in the second half, perhaps, in which Orwell's tramping adventures over several years are spliced together into a single narrative, but much in evidence in the Parisian sequences that open the book. As early as the second chapter, for example, Orwell is regaling us with a monologue about a brothel visit from one of the regulars at the local bistro that looks as if it came straight out of a volume of Second Empire pornography ('And then I fell upon her like a tiger! Ah, the joy, the incomparable rapture of that time!' etc.). The reader is clearly intended to take the Parisian chapters at face value, and yet the list of comments Orwell scribbled in the margin of a copy presented to a Suffolk friend introduces a faint note of ambiguity. The trip to the offices of a communist secret society 'happened very much as described'; the description of going without food for three days is marked 'This all happened'; but the third chapter carries the annotation 'Succeeding chapters not actually autobiography, but drawn from what I have seen.' By the time Orwell got round to writing an introduction to the French translation in 1934, this tocsin clangs even louder. Everything he records did take place at one time or another, he assures his readers, but the characters he describes 'are intended more as representative types'.

As well as its mild hint of stage-management, *Down and Out* offers another puzzle. This is the question of Orwell's persona, and the information supplied throughout the text about its hero. Like the protagonists of his novels, the Orwell of his tramping adventures and exploits among the Parisian lowlife is an isolated figure, detached, out on the margins of a society in whose blandishments and amenities he takes no interest. If he is not without friends – Boris, his fellow waiter, various tramps with whom he strikes up a temporary acquaintance – no one should doubt the solitariness of his gaze. And the narrator of *Down and Out* is not just isolated; he is also imperilled. On neither side of the Channel is there a safety net. Running out of money in Paris, he simply starves. Back in England, and discovering that a job looking after a congenital idiot promised him by his friend 'B' has fallen through, he has no option but to take to the streets. It would be impossible to gather from this that the Orwell who lived in Paris in 1928–9 did so in close proximity to his maternal aunt, Nellie Limouzin, at whose house he was a regular guest, or that the Orwell who returned to England at the end of his stay immediately made a beeline for his parents' home in Southwold. Orwell needs these devices to make the book work, to introduce a genuine element of uncertainty and existential threat, but they involve several distinctive departures from the reality of his own life. Although he did at one time take a holiday job looking after a backward boy, 'B' seems to have been a figment of his imagination.

If *Down and Out* is an example of Orwell's habit of leavening reportage with some of the techniques of fiction, then *A Clergyman's Daughter* plays the trick in reverse, using a novel as the binding agent for a large amount of disguised autobiography. The first eighty pages or so offer a dense, naturalistic and bitingly funny account of backwoods Suffolk life in the town of 'Knype Hill' in the early 1930s, here represented as a kind of sink of backbiting and gossipy intrigue. Several unstoppable forces are conspiring to drag its twenty-something heroine down: they range from an exacting clerical father for whom she routinely drudges and the environment through which she wanders to the exaggerated sense of duty which leads her to turn out uncomplainingly for early-morning communion, anoint old ladies' legs with liniment and spend long hours manufacturing costumes for church pageants. Then, in the wake of a late-evening encounter with the town's solitary bohemian scamp, a middle-aged roué named Mr Warburton, Dorothy's world is turned upside down. Returning to consciousness a week later in the Old Kent Road, wearing unfamiliar clothes but with two shillings and sixpence in her pocket, she discovers that she has lost her memory.

By chance this resurfacing is witnessed by a band of vagrants on their way to the Kentish hop fields. Within moments Dorothy agrees to join them, hands over the half-crown to their leader, Nobby, and is on her way by tram to Bromley. Existing for several weeks in a state of semi-somnambulism, she is jolted out of her trance by the memory of her fellow tramps discussing a tabloid newspaper story about the disappearance, late at night and in apparently doubtful circumstances, of a 'rector's daughter'. Retrieving a copy of a Sunday scandal sheet that has featured the case, Dorothy is finally able to piece the fragments of her recent life back together again: 'For it was strange, but she no longer had any shadow of doubt that this girl whom she was reading about was herself.' Getting no reply from the letter she immediately sends to her father, and aware that the hop-picking season will soon be over, Dorothy gravitates to London, runs through the small stock of money she has earned in the fields, spends a chilly night sleeping on a bench in Trafalgar Square and ends up in a police court after begging from 'a nasty old lady with a face like a horse' who promptly summons the nearest policeman and puts her in charge.

By this time her father has stirred himself to act and Dorothy, rescued by her aristocratic cousin Sir Thomas Hare, is swiftly inducted into the life of a private schoolmistress in west London. On the very day that she is sacked by her Dickensian employer, Mr Warburton arrives bearing the news that the gossip responsible for her troubles has been exposed as a fantasist and she can return to Knype Hill with the public behind her. Of the many questions stirred up by Orwell's picaresque narrative, the most obvious is: what exactly happens to Dorothy? Sensing that the reader will need a full explanation of how she comes to be sitting on a street corner in a district of working-class London, Orwell offers the following:

> The thing that had happened to her was commonplace enough – almost every week one reads in the newspapers of a similar case. A man disappears from home, is lost sight of for days or weeks, and presently fetches up at a police station or hospital, with no notion of who he is or where he has come from. As a rule, it is impossible to tell how he has spent the intervening time; he has been wandering, presumably, in some hypnotic or somnambulistic state in which he has nevertheless been able to pass for normal.

In Dorothy's case, we are assured, the one certain fact about the eight days she has spent somewhere between Knype Hill and the Old Kent Road is that she has been robbed: the clothes she is wearing are not her own and her gold cross is missing. The encounter with the tramps has come at exactly the wrong moment: 'when Nobby accosted her, she was already on the road to recovery; and if she had been properly cared for, her memory might have come back to her within a few days or even hours.' As it is she is left in a peculiar state: her mind is 'potentially normal' but not yet able to get to grips with the question of her own identity.

None of this, it has to be said, sounds especially plausible. If, at the moment in the hop-pickers' hut when Dorothy turns up the copy of *Pippin's Weekly* with its flaring headline ('PASSION DRAMA IN COUNTRY RECTORY') and is brought dramatically back to earth, she is able to remember everything in her life up until the evening with Mr Warburton, why can't she remember the lost eight days? (These are never referred to again, and don't seem to trouble her.) And why, having been unable to make contact with her father, doesn't she seek out some family friend or London-bound acquaintance rather than assuming that her destiny lies on the streets? The suspicion looms that Orwell neither knows what has happened to Dorothy nor is particularly interested in the circumstances of her departure: all he requires is a mechanism that can transport her from Knype Hill to a peripatetic life in Kent and London based on his own adventures in the two years after he came back from Paris. There is a way, too, in which, after the opening section, he sometimes seems to lose interest in her as a character, such is his eagerness to impart hop-picking tips – the only two things capable of getting the dirt off your hands are mud and hop juice – or the application of the London vagrancy laws. By the end, the reader will suspect that it is Orwell as much as Dorothy who has 'gone native'.

The young teacher with his pupils at the Hawthorns School for Boys, Middlesex, 1932.

4

STATUS ANXIETY

*A CLERGYMAN'S DAUGHTER • KEEP THE
ASPIDISTRA FLYING • THE COMPLETE POETRY •
COMING UP FOR AIR • 'CONFESSIONS OF A
BOOK REVIEWER'*

Orwell's literary career proper began in January 1933 when *Down and Out in Paris in London* was published by the firm of Victor Gollancz. Worried that some of the material might embarrass his intensely conservative parents, he had originally volunteered the pseudonym 'X'. Wiser counsels prevailed, and the name on the title page was 'George Orwell'. The jettisoning of 'Eric Blair' is sometimes seen as a symbolic act in which Orwell abandoned his bygone life with the aim of transforming himself into a different kind of person, but the reality is more prosaic. 'George Orwell', which combined the name of the reigning monarch and the principal Suffolk river, was only one among a number of potential aliases – the others were 'P.S. Burton', 'Kenneth Miles' and 'H. Lewis Allways' – offered up for Gollancz's inspection. Meanwhile, Orwell continued to sign book reviews as 'E.A. Blair' for some time afterwards. Neither was the throwing-over of his baptismal name any kind of a career move. None of the twenty-something old Etonians making a name for themselves had any idea that the author of *Down and Out* was their one-time schoolfellow, and Cyril Connolly's rediscovery of his old friend had to wait until 1935.

Once established as a writer, Orwell moved fast: his first three novels followed in a bare thirty-six months. But none of the four books he published between 1933 and 1936 earned him very much money – the advance for *Down and Out* was £40; the three novels brought £100 each – and his financial position in the early to mid-1930s was frequently precarious. Forced to supplement his meagre income with day jobs, he spent much of 1932–3 teaching in flyblown private schools in west London, and from the autumn of 1934 to the beginning of 1936 served behind the counter of a Hampstead bookshop. The intervening nine months found him in Southwold recuperating from a serious bout of pneumonia and writing *A Clergyman's Daughter*. This period in his life was brought to an end by a burgeoning relationship with Eileen O'Shaughnessy, whom he met in mid-1935 and married a year later. But the years that preceded it were not a happy time in Orwell's life, and his dissatisfaction leaches into the novels. Although they have very different themes and settings, *Burmese Days*, *A Clergyman's Daughter* and *Keep the Aspidistra Flying* are all, in their various ways, about middle-class people on their uppers, trying to keep their heads above water in an increasingly hostile world.

People like their creator, in fact. Several of Orwell's letters from the early 1930s show just how well aware he was of the shakiness of his situation. A note from mid-1931 to Brenda Salkeld, written the day after his twenty-eighth birthday, reckons up his earnings from the time he joined the Burma police nearly nine years before. From the angle of the aspiring writer, it made depressing reading: 'Writing' has produced about £100, his 'present job' – we have no idea what this was, unless Orwell is referring to the private tutoring that occupied him in parts of 1930–1 – about £220, the Burma police around £2,000, 'dishwashing about £20', other odd jobs about the same. Brenda would notice, Orwell concludes, 'that the only profession I have made anything appreciable at was the only one I wholeheartedly loathed'. There are other hints that his early life was strewn with anxiety about money. Mr Wilkes in 'Such, Such Were the Joys' is forever warning his pupils that the fate of an exam-failer is to become 'a little office boy at £40 a year', which just happens to be Gollancz's advance for Orwell's first book. Avril recalled that when she and her mother visited him in hospital in December 1933, the by-then delirious patient was babbling about money, to the extent that he seemed to believe there was some hidden under the pillow.

Significantly, Orwell's literary interests were leading him the same way. His great discovery here in the early 1930s was George Gissing (1857–1903), and in particular *New Grub Street* (1891), a novel set on the lower rungs of the late-Victorian book world whose subject might be described as the emotional consequences of money's absence. Edwin Reardon, its diffident and nerve-racked hero, has a freak success with a novel. On the strength of it he marries the beautiful and socially ambitious Amy, who imagines that she has hitched herself to a genius. Instead, Reardon's muse deserts him. He begins to suffer from writer's block – the scenes in which he wanders round the London streets trying to cudgel his brain into action have a dreadful tang of authenticity – and the money runs out. In the end a disillusioned Amy goes back to live with her mother, while her husband takes a job as a clerk. There is a revealing scene in which Reardon, come to plead his case, arrives in his usual shabby suit. Amy, initially prepared to take him back, is disgusted. As Gissing notes: 'Had Reardon been practical man enough to prepare by hook or by crook a decent suit of clothes for this interview, that ridiculous trifle might have made all the difference in what was to result.' Some of the dialogue between Gordon and his girlfriend Rosemary in *Keep the Aspidistra Flying* strikes exactly the same note, in particular Gordon's insistence that Rosemary would consent to sleep with him provided he earned a decent salary.

On the other hand, the hardships experienced by Gissing's mostly down-at-heel cast are rarely those of outright degradation. This is a shabby-genteel poverty whose distinguishing marks are embarrassment and compromise. In much the same way, none of the characters in *A Clergyman's Daughter* and *Keep the Aspidistra Flying* actually starves. The Hares and the Comstocks are people who have come down in the world: Dorothy is the great-granddaughter of a baronet; Gordon is the grandson of a self-made plutocrat. Behind them both lies the fading grandeur of a lost Victorian world of money and social position. Half a century later all the certainty of their ancestors has crumbled into dust. Dorothy's relative security will disappear the moment her elderly father dies. The only barrier between Gordon and penury is his job at the bookshop. His life, consequently, consists of a permanent battle to remain respectable: rationing his cigarettes, inking the bare skin that gleams through the holes in his socks, agonising over the likely cost of taking Rosemary out for a meal. The abyss can be glimpsed on every side, and a single false step may send him stumbling over the edge.

The status anxiety that threatens to undermine the protagonists of Orwell's 1930s fiction has a physical dimension. Many of the working-class characters in *A Clergyman's Daughter* have a kind of resourceful, animal vigour. Dorothy's travelling companion Nobby, for example, can be found spending the night in a nest of sodden grass, yet 'his coarse, simian face never lost its warm, pink colour. He was one of those red-haired people who seem to glow with an inner radiance that warms not only themselves but the surrounding air.' Most of the vagrants on their way to Kent are in a state of permanent exhaustion, the exception being Nobby, 'whom nothing could tire'. Nobby's vitality is in sharp contrast to most of Orwell's middle-class protagonists. Dorothy, though described as 'strong and shapely', is let down by her face – a 'thin, blonde, unremarkable kind of face, with pale eyes, and a nose just a shade too long'. Additionally, there are crow's feet round her eyes and her mouth, in repose, 'looked tired'. The five-foot-seven-inch Gordon is 'a small frail figure, with delicate bones and fretful movements', not yet thirty but 'moth-eaten already'. Like Dorothy, Gordon's face does him no favours: 'Hair mouse-coloured and unkempt, mouth unamiable, eyes hazel inclining to green.'

Or there is Julia, Gordon's dutiful, put-upon sister, 'a tall, ungainly girl with a thin face and a neck just a little too long' who 'reminds one irresistibly of a goose'. Set against Orwell's upper-class characters, Dorothy, Gordon and Julia look oddly insubstantial. Ravelston, Gordon's well-meaning patron, transparently based on Orwell's friend and professional sponsor Sir Richard Rees, editor of the *Adelphi*, is 'very tall, with a lean, wide-shouldered body and the typical lounging grace of the upper-class youth'. Introducing Hermione, Ravelston's equally well-bred girlfriend, Orwell can scarcely contain himself, for Hermione, whose prejudices include a belief that 'the working classes smell' – a shibboleth that hung over Orwell's own childhood – has shoulders that seem to 'rise out of her clothes like a mermaid rising from the sea' and skin and hair that are 'somehow warm and sleepy, like a wheatfield in the sun'. Even the minor upper-class walk-ons possess this quality. However contemptuously Orwell may regard the ambiguous young man who comes to browse in the bookshop where he works, he is forced to concede that he is a 'nice-looking boy'. As with Hermione, the attraction seems to derive from a kind of elemental sheen: 'The skin on the back of his neck was as silky-smooth as the inside of a shell.' All this, Gordon decides, is simply one of the advantages of wealth: 'You can't have a skin like that under five hundred a year. A sort of charm he had, a glamour, like all moneyed people.'

If Orwell's middle-class characters seem physically lacking when compared to well-heeled *jeunes premiers* such as Ravelston and the boy in the bookshop, then there also a hint that they are morally inferior as well. Gordon's attitude to Ravelston is relatively complex. On the one hand, although the proprietor of the radical journal *Antichrist* is happy to print his poems and shepherd his solitary collection into print, Gordon is always drawing attention to the gulf between them, forever harping on about his lack of money and 'talking with self-pitiful detail of the bloodiness of life on two quid a week'. On the other, he adores Ravelston, is proud of their friendship and detects in him qualities that are absent in himself: 'Ravelston had not merely a charm of manner, but also a kind of fundamental decency, a graceful attitude to life, which Gordon scarcely encountered elsewhere.' The sting comes in the sentence that follows. 'Undoubtedly it was bound up with the fact that Ravelston was rich.' Ultimately, Orwell will qualify this judgement, insist that in some ways Ravelston 'was not even like a moneyed person', that 'the fatty degeneration of spirit that goes with wealth had missed him, or he had escaped it by a conscious effort', but still there lurks a suspicion that it is Ravelston's £2,000 a year that makes him the highly attractive person he is.

◎

This absorption in the frailties of the English petit bourgeois is given an even sharper focus by Orwell's final 1930s novel, *Coming Up for Air* (1939), in which he turns his customary class perspective on its head. As the son of a small tradesman in an Oxfordshire town, George Bowling is thoroughly aware of the value of money, but much less hung up about it and much more prepared to let the future take care of itself. Hilda, his gloomy and joyless wife, on the other hand, is a deep-dyed middle-class neurotic, forever worrying herself about unpaid school fees and rising grocery bills. The reader first glimpses her 'glooming behind the tea pot, in her usual state of alarm and dismay, because the *News Chronicle* had announced the price of butter was going up, or something'. A keen student of social distinctions, Bowling attributes his wife's anxiety to an upbringing in an impoverished middle-class household clinging desperately to its gentility: 'Hilda's often told me that the first thing she can remember is a ghastly feeling that there was never enough money for anything.' Their early married life is consequently hedged around by 'that ghastly glooming about money! The milk bill! The coal bill ... We've lived our life together to the tune of "Next week we'll be in the workhouse."'

Once again, the chasm that yawns between Bowling and his wife has a physical dimension. George, though weighing in at something over fourteen stone and unable to see various parts of his body when standing erect, is comfortable in his skin, happy with the way he looks, untroubled about his ability to deal with anything the world throws at him: 'I haven't such a bad face,' he insists, and with his false teeth in, 'I probably don't look my age, which is forty-five.' Hilda, alternatively, though six years younger, is ageing fast. Bowling, coolly appraising her over the breakfast table in the novel's opening chapter, decides that she has got 'very thin, and rather wizened, with a perpetual brooding, worried look in her eyes, and when she's more upset than usual she's got a trick of humping her shoulders and folding her arms across her breast, like an old gypsy woman over her fire'. If Bowling's interests are those of the average pleasure-seeking *homme moyen sensuel* – drink, women, large meals, comfortable repose – then, mysteriously, what Hilda lacks is 'any kind of joy in life, any kind of interest in things for their own sake'. All this, her husband diagnoses, is a result of the way in which she was brought up. To be born into her social background is to acquire 'a fixed idea not only that one always *is* hard-up but that it's one's duty to be miserable about it'.

Seen in this light, *A Clergyman's Daughter* and *Keep the Aspidistra Flying* are novels about socio-economic insecurity, highly acute and unrelenting despatches from a type of middle-class life that is under attack: an existence in which most kinds of human enjoyment are being quietly eclipsed by anxieties about money and keeping up appearances. Nowhere is this assault on bourgeois values more obvious, perhaps, than in *A Clergyman's Daughter*'s opening section, which tracks Dorothy's progress around the Suffolk market town of Knype Hill. Where exactly is this hotbed of spite and gossip located? Although Orwell makes a perfunctory attempt or two to disguise his tracks – the town is described as being inland and dominated by its sugar beet factory – it is clear, more or less from the opening chapter, that this is Southwold, which, although situated on the coast and dominated by the Adnams brewery, shares Kynpe Hill's topography almost to the last brick. 'After about two hundred yards the High Street forked, forming a tiny market-place, adorned with a pump, now defunct, and a worm-eaten pair of stocks.' With the exception of the stocks, which can be found outside the local church, this is Southwold to the life.

Orwell's sister Avril believed that he 'loathed Southwold', and detested its gossip-mongering, ultra-conservative small-town atmosphere. Certainly, *A Clergyman's Daughter* pulls no punches. Still in the high street, Orwell notes that 'It was one of those sleepy, old-fashioned streets that look so ideally peaceful on a casual visit and so very different when you live in them and have an enemy or a creditor behind every window.' There is space, too, for Avril's own involvement in the life of the town, for before very long her brother turns his gaze on an up-market emporium called 'Ye Olde Tea Shoppe'. This has a 'revolting curly roof like that of a Chinese joss-house', is filled with idle middle-class ladies come to trade scandal and discuss last night's bridge party over their coffee cups, and is clearly poking fraternal fun at an establishment named 'The Copper Kettle', over which Avril herself presided a few yards down the high street from the Blair family home at Montague House.

But the identification of Knype Hill with Southwold becomes even more unignorable a paragraph later. Orwell returned to his parents' house early in January 1934 to convalesce and continue with his novel, a scant few pages of which were complete at the time he was admitted to hospital. From his bedroom window at the lower end of the high street he was perfectly placed to monitor the electioneering that took place in the town a few weeks later in preparation for the Lowestoft constituency by-election. This contest, won by the Conservative candidate Pierse Loftus, a director of Adnams, over his Labour opponent with a majority of 1,900 votes, is faithfully reproduced in *A Clergyman's Daughter*. Loftus is disguised as 'Mr

Blifil-Gordon', owner of the beet factory ('Who'll save Britain from the Reds? BLIFIL-GORDON! Who'll put the Beer back into your Pot? BLIFIL-GORDON!'), and given a lisping son named 'Walph', described as 'an epicene youth of twenty given to writing sub-Eliot *vers libre*' – a gross libel of the achievements of Loftus's son Murrough, whose first book of poems appeared later that year.

What had the Loftuses, father and son, done to annoy Orwell? Or indeed any other of the residents of Knype Hill brought into *A Clergyman's Daughter*'s opening pages? These include the tight-fisted Miss Mayfill, whose contribution to the parish fête are two handle-less chamber pots, and Mrs Semprill, doyenne of the local backbiters. Even the working classes seem to fail him here in rural Suffolk: Mrs Pither, whom Dorothy visits in her stinking cottage, is an elderly drudge whose religious beliefs are based on a blue-skies-deferred acceptance of her lot redeemed by an afterlife where 'every little bit of suffering, you gets it back a hundredfold and a thousandfold'. Why did Orwell hate Southwold – where he spent long stretches of time in the 1930s and met two of his closest women-friends – so much? The answer seems to be that he regarded it as a symbol of everything he most disliked about English middle-class life – a dislike that was made yet more extravagant by the fact that he was a part of that life himself.

This tendency is all the more marked in *Keep the Aspidistra Flying*, which takes some of these anxieties and gives them an even sharper twist. Gordon Comstock is a struggling poet, the author of a single, highly praised collection, who has thrown over a promising career as a copywriter in an advertising agency owing to his contempt for the 'money-god' and come to rest in Mr McKechnie's Hampstead bookshop. Here he spends his time silently despising both the stock and the people who come to purchase it; home life consists of a shabby bedsitting room in an establishment administered by the ever-vigilant Mrs Wisbeach, marked down as 'one of those malignant respectable women who keep lodging-houses'. When not dodging Mrs Wisbeach or lounging miserably in the shop, Gordon is sustained by his relationships with Ravelston and his girlfriend Rosemary; evenings not spent in their company are frittered away in his room pretending to work on a long poem entitled *London Pleasures*, a projected 2,000 lines in rhyme royal describing a day out in London, two years in the writing, which has now 'simply fallen apart into a series of fragments' and will pretty clearly never be finished, let alone published.

Rosemary, naturally, is cut from the same, frayed middle-class cloth as her devitalised boyfriend; girlish-looking, but with three symbolical white hairs on her crown which she declines to pull out: 'She still thought of herself as a very young girl, and so did everybody else. Yet if you looked closely, the marks of time were plain enough on her face.' Gordon, meanwhile, turns out to be his own worst enemy, sensitive and insecure, resolved to bite every hand held out to feed him and making a point of detaching himself from what he regards as a corrupt and self-serving literary world. Arriving at the house of an influential critic to find that a promised tea party has been postponed and that the host has forgotten to tell him, he instantly fires off a furious letter that will sever their relationship for all time. This downward spiral quickens up when he receives an unexpected cheque for $50 from an American literary magazine, goes on a terrific bender in Soho, is arrested for being drunk and disorderly, spends a night in the cells and is sacked from his job.

Relocated to an even seedier bedsit in working-class Lambeth and employed to run a downmarket twopenny library where the display cards advertise such categories as 'sex', 'crime' and 'wild west', he is visited by Rosemary, who announces, sometime after their encounter, that she is pregnant. Will Gordon stick by his principles and abandon Rosemary to her fate or do the decent thing, here in the morally disapproving 1930s where the arrival of an illegitimate baby is enough to ruin its mother's life? In the end, he swallows his pride, goes back to the agency, marries Rosemary, installs the pair of them in a tiny flat off the Edgware Road ('a dull quarter and rather a slummy street, but it was convenient for the centre of London') and ruefully acknowledges that the houseplant of the title – a symbol of the respectable bourgeois destiny he has tried so hard to resist – has finally gained the upper hand.

There are two obvious questions to be asked of a novel of which Anthony Powell, detecting its most significant literary influence, later pronounced that 'the Gissing had to stop'. The first is narrowly professional: what kind of poet is Gordon Comstock? Certainly not a very successful one – *Mice*, his solitary volume of verse, has been remaindered after selling a paltry 153 copies. But where does he stand in terms of the complex aesthetic currents of the 1930s? A critic is supposed to have said of *Mice* that it represents 'a welcome relief from the Sitwell [i.e. high-modernist] school'. Yet the most substantial clue lies in the poem that Gordon can be found meditating upon in the opening chapter:

Sharply the menacing wind sweeps over
The bending poplars, newly bare,
And the dark ribbons of the chimneys
Veer downward; flicked by whips of air,
Torn posters flutter.

Subsequently 'St Andrew's Day, 1935', as Orwell titled it when it appeared in the *Adelphi*, goes on to descry a bleak urban vista of anxious clerks worrying about their jobs and household expenses while they kneel before 'The lord of all, the money-god / Who owns us, blood and hand and brain' and who, among other interventions, 'lays the sleek, estranging shield / Between the lover and his bride' – probably the first reference to a contraceptive in English poetry.

Gordon, on the evidence of 'St Andrew's Day', is the same kind of poet as his creator: in thrall to Eliot and occupying a position halfway between the Georgian poetry of the period 1910–25 and the

Auden-inflected demotic that followed it. Orwell's career as a versifier is often overlooked by critics, and yet he produced enough poems to fill a small volume – see Dione Venables's *George Orwell: The Complete Poetry* (2015) – reportage from the tramping days, *vers d'occasion* ('Memories of the Blitz', 1944), love poems to his Suffolk girlfriends Brenda Salkeld and Eleanor Jaques and a great deal else. Read chronologically, his forty-seven-poem life's work falls into several clearly demarcated groups: patriotic juvenilia (his first appearance in print was a poem in a local newspaper encouraging young men to enlist in the Great War); teenage effusions to Jacintha Buddicom; a series of verses written during or shortly after his time in Burma; downbeat exercises in 1930s miserabilism. The style is almost purposefully old-fashioned, regular as clockwork and impeccably scanned, and the models – Eliot excepted – are nearly always bygone exemplars such as Walter de la Mare and W.H. Davies.

As for the impulse which inspired this slim oeuvre, composed in school holidays, on the boat home from Rangoon or on spare surfaces in London lodging houses, in some ways the context is quite as beguiling as the poems themselves. The early twentieth century was a time at which, as Penelope Fitzgerald once put it, the English people 'still liked poetry', when sales of John Masefield's *Collected Poems* weighed in at 80,000 copies and the ongoing war between modernism and Georgian-style traditionalism was fought out from one newspaper arts section to the next. Then came the romantic haze that hung over the memory of all the young men who had died in Flanders ('How George would have loved to have been a poet killed in the First World War,' a friend once remarked). To the twenty-something neophyte who wanted to 'be a writer' in the age of Ramsay MacDonald and Stanley Baldwin, poetry seemed every bit as seductive a form as the novel, and the number of Orwell's contemporaries who began their careers in verse takes in everyone from Graham Greene (*Babbling April*, 1924) to Patrick Hamilton.

In most cases the virus burnt itself out at a comparatively early stage. Evelyn Waugh's elder brother Alec, for example, published a single volume of poetry (*Resentment*, 1918) and then seems to have given up the medium altogether. One of the fascinations of Orwell's ambitions as a poet, however, is how long they survived. As late as the early 1930s, he can be found writing to his agent, Leonard Moore, about his own version of *London Pleasures* – about as backward-looking a project as an interwar-era literary man could possibly conceive. All this adds up. In one of the few articles he ever wrote that touches on sport – a review of Edmund Blunden's *Cricket Country* (1944) – Orwell confesses to once having conducted a 'hopeless love affair with cricket': the same could be said of his attitude to verse. Not that 'hopeless' is quite the right adjective for a relationship that lasted from early childhood to the year of his death. In fact, the reader who comes fresh to Orwell's poems will very soon divine quite how much the form meant to him and how considerable are the kind of effects he was able to bring off when his emotions were truly stirred. It is significant, for example, that his encounter with an Italian militiaman in Spain, with its terrific final quatrain – 'But the thing that I saw in your face / No power can disinherit: / No bomb that ever burst / Shatters the crystal spirit' – should be written up as a poem rather than set down in prose: the implication is that Orwell thought poetry a better vehicle for conveying this mixture of personal reaction and universal truth.

Keep the Aspidistra Flying's second puzzle is what might be called the 'spoiled naturalism' of its finale. In normal circumstances, naturalist fiction involves the unhindered working-out of natural forces, in which the end is implied by the beginning. You just know that Gervaise Macquart, the uncomplaining heroine of Zola's *L'Assommoir*, will die in poverty, just as you immediately deduce that Studs Lonigan, the hero of James T. Farrell's *Judgment Day* (1935), won't survive his last illness: the odds are too heavily stacked against them, and a change of tack would betray the animating spirit of everything that has gone before. *Aspidistra*, on the other hand, cheerfully abandons all the principles established in its preceding chapters for the prospect of a happy ending. The problem about this recalibration of the novel's scale of values is that it fails to square with what we know of Gordon, whose entire career thus far has consisted of throwing over promising opportunities and letting people down. In coming to rest in the Lambeth backstreets, he is at least being true to himself. There is satisfaction, too, in the mundane trappings of his life. As he reflects:

> In this place he could have been happy if only people would let him alone. It was a place where you *could* be happy, in a sluttish way. To spend your days in meaningless mechanical work that could be slovened through in a kind of coma; to come home and light the fire when you had any coal (there were sixpenny bags at the grocer's) and get the stuffy little attic warm; to sit over a squalid meal of bacon, bread and tea ... it was the kind of life he wanted.

So why marry Rosemary? In the hands of a Zola or a Farrell, *Keep the Aspidistra Flying* would doubtless have ended with Gordon still frowsting in his Lambeth attic and Rosemary despatched to a home for unmarried mothers. In Orwell's defence, nearly all English novelists south of Hardy end up making this kind of compromise – the most obvious example is *Great Expectations*, whose ending goes against the grain of nearly everything that has preceded it – merely to keep the reader on their side. On the other hand, it may be that the explanation is more personal. Orwell began work on the book in the autumn of 1934. Progress was comparatively slow, and some of his letters to friends suggest a degree of uncertainty over its form; writing to Eleanor in January 1935 he notes that 'After all my researches – which, however, were not wasted – I have decided to do the new one as a novel, after all, as that gives me a freer hand.' But its later stages coincided with the start of his relationship with Eileen. To Eileen's biographer Sylvia Topp, the note of uplift that typifies *Aspidistra*'s final stretch and the promise of this new love affair are naturally connected: 'As Orwell was writing these closing pages, he was becoming more optimistic in his personal life. Eileen had agreed to marry him, and they were thinking ahead about having their own child.' For the ardent lover, plotting a new future far away from London, naturalism could only go so far.

◎

In later life, Orwell took against *A Clergyman's Daughter* and *Keep the Aspidistra Flying*, claimed that the former was 'bollix' and that the latter had been written simply to get his hands on Gollancz's £100 advance: neither book was allowed into a collected edition of his work published shortly before his death, and no reprint appeared until a decade after he was gone. This blanket disparagement is odd, for both novels are not only intriguing works in their own right but, as Orwell must have known, significant marker-flags on the path to *Nineteen Eighty-Four*; *Aspidistra*, in particular, is highly prefigurative of the world of Winston Smith. Like Winston, with his varicose veins and his reluctance to join in the early-morning PE sessions, Gordon is a frail, puny specimen. Like Winston, he suffers agonies over carefully hoarded cigarettes and the lack of razor blades. Even more striking, perhaps, is his connection to some of *Nineteen Eighty-Four*'s thematic architecture. Just as Winston will cheerfully inform Julia that 'We are the dead', so Gordon laments the lack of vitality in his poems: 'My poems are dead because I'm dead,' he assures a sympathetic Ravelston. 'You're dead. I'm dead. Dead people in a dead world.'

It is the same with Gordon's emotional life, which reaches its highest point out in the countryside. On a Thames Valley excursion with Rosemary, the couple sit arm in arm as sunshine suddenly irradiates the winter landscape: 'As the clouds melted away a widening yellow beam slid swiftly across the valley, gilding everything in its path. Grass that had been dull green shone suddenly emerald.' This is uncannily prophetic of Winston's *plein air* frolics with Julia, conducted in rural hideaways where the sunlight, 'filtering through innumerable leaves, was still hot on their faces' and the song of a solitary thrush drives all disagreeable speculations from his mind. And yet the strongest link between the world of Willowbed Road, NW, where Gordon spends most of his leisure hours, and the nightmare landscapes inhabited by Winston Smith comes in the ever-present threat of surveillance. If Winston is menaced by telescreens and hidden microphones, then Gordon finds himself constantly eavesdropped on and monitored by his landlady: 'It was queer how furtively you had to live in Mrs Wisbeach's house. You had the feeling that she was always watching you; and indeed she was given to tiptoeing up and downstairs at all hours, in the hope of catching the lodgers up to mischief.'

But there is another way in which *Keep the Aspidistra Flying* foreshadows some of the political positions that Orwell would formulate in the following decade. The middle-class people at large in it are comparatively rootless, detached from the world of their upbringing in a way that their Victorian forebears were not. Many an interwarera English novel peddles this theme: the desiccated accountant Mr Smeeth, for example, in J.B. Priestley's *Angel Pavement* (1930) is taken aback by the gulf that lies between himself and his children, 'not simply because they belonged to a younger generation, but because they belonged to a younger generation that existed in a different world . . . They were the product of a changing civilisation, creatures of a post-war world.' But Mr Smeeth himself is aware of his own deracination, the sense that the certainties that attended his early manhood have all but disappeared.

Orwell's awareness of some of the political consequences of a fraying middle class is a feature of a round-up review of a quartet of dystopian novels he wrote for *Tribune* in July 1940. The four novels are Jack London's *The Iron Heel* (1908), H.G. Wells's *The Sleeper*

Awakes (1910), Aldous Huxley's *Brave New World* (1932) and *The Secret of the League* (1907) by the much less well-known Ernest Bramah. Although Orwell supplies shrewd analyses of the first three – he finds Huxley's hedonistic futurism unconvincing, on the grounds that 'A ruling class has got to have a strict morality, a quasi-religious belief in itself, a *mystique*' – the novel that seems most to interest him is the fourth. The fascination of *The Secret of the League*, he assures us, stems from its middle-class view of the class struggle: 'As a political forecast it is trivial, but it is of great interest for the light it casts on the struggling middle classes.'

Bramah's villains are an incoming Labour government whose members, rather than introducing red-blooded socialism, merely operate capitalism for their own benefit. Ranged against it is a secret conspiracy of the upper and middle classes, which in the aftermath of a civil war, seizes the reins of power, abolishes the trade unions and establishes an autocratic non-parliamentary regime. To Orwell, the most curious aspect of the novel is its 'good-natured' tone. Why, he wonders, should such a 'decent and kindly' writer as Bramah take such pleasure in the crushing of the proletariat? The answer is that this middle-class revolt against socialism is 'simply the reaction of a struggling class which felt itself menaced not so much in its economic position as its way of life'. As for the literary context, 'One can see the same purely social antagonism to the working class in an earlier writer of much greater calibre, George Gissing.' The review ends with a dig at 'Socialist propaganda', whose 'constant baiting of the "petit bourgeois" has a lot to answer for'. In the status anxiety of the middle classes, Orwell seems to be saying, lie the roots of fascism.

◎

Orwell's own status anxiety seems to have persisted almost until death. As late as May 1946, nine months after *Animal Farm* had established his reputation for all time, he can be found entertaining – or perhaps only alarming – the readers of *Tribune* with an essay entitled 'Confessions of a Book Reviewer'. It is one of the funniest, and also one of the most revealing pieces that he ever wrote, and all the more pointed for its blatant connection to his own professional life. The hapless hack, entombed in his bedsitting room with the cigarette smoke rising to the ceiling, is not quite Orwell himself, but it is near enough to his life in the mid-1930s to give the 'confession' a dreadful resonance.

The sketch begins with our hero, a man of thirty-five who 'looks fifty', is bald, has varicose veins and wears spectacles, staring bleakly at a paper-strewn desk at which he should have started work two hours ago. Even had he kept to his schedule the pursuit would have been futile, Orwell helpfully glosses, owing to the 'almost continuous ringing of the telephone bell, the yells of the baby, the rattle of an electric drill out in the street, and the heavy boots of his creditors thumping up and down the stairs'. Before him on the desk – in fact, half-hidden beneath the pile of papers – are five books which arrived four days before but which he was prevented from opening for forty-eight hours by 'moral paralysis'. Their titles are *Palestine at the Cross Roads*, *Scientific Dairy Farming*, *A Short History of European Democracy*, *Tribal Customs in Portuguese East Africa* and a novel called *It's Nicer Lying Down*, 'probably included by mistake'.

By this stage the piece has revealed itself as a burlesque. It is probable that no book reviewer was ever given such a miscellaneous set of volumes to appraise. All Orwell's characteristic tricks of exaggeration and weighted diction are well to the fore. Never mind the 'moral paralysis'; the prospect of having to read them affects his phantom hack 'like the prospect of eating cold ground-rice pudding flavoured with castor oil'. And yet eventually, with only a few moments to spare before next lunchtime's deadline, amid a torrent of bogus praise ('a book that no one should miss ... something memorable on every page' etc.) and with the cigarette smoke growing thicker by the minute, the work will be done, even if the reviewer is conscious that 'he is pouring his immortal spirit down the drain, a pint at a time'.

Inevitably, Orwell has a serious point to make. The business of putting words on paper is, he implies, a romantic activity, a pursuit of a long-meditated creative ideal in which failure hurts ('And yet with what high hopes this downtrodden, nerve-wracked creature started his career, only a few years ago'). The difficulty in reviewing the work of one's peers, however, lies in the mediocrity of so much of what gets published. 'Until one has some kind of professional relationship with books, one does not discover how bad the majority of them are,' Orwell insists. There is no place for objective standards, for once the reviewer has decided that a routine thriller is exceptionally good, what is there left to say about Shakespeare? An earlier essay, 'In Defence of the Novel', written for the *New English Weekly* a decade before, canvasses the need for a kind of critical spring balance capable of weighing an elephant and a flea simultaneously. Here Orwell notes that it is impossible to mention books in bulk without 'grossly over-praising' the majority of them. None of 'Confessions' is calculated to boost the average literary man or woman's esteem, for its message is that nine out of ten books are worthless, that a critic is not much more than a prostitute destined to become the 'crushed figure' of the smoke-laden bedsitter. All this chimes with Orwell's wider view of his craft. He once maintained that a writer is like a house sparrow: tolerated until it makes a nuisance of itself, and then briskly suppressed.

With Eileen and POUM comrades on the Huesca Front, 1937.

5

POLITICS

*THE ROAD TO WIGAN PIER • HOMAGE
TO CATALONIA • COMING UP FOR AIR*

Orwell came late to politics. In an intensely politicised age, which discouraged fence-sitting and preached the advantages of 'commitment' to the up-and-coming writer, he was the tardiest of slow starters. This may seem a surprising claim to make of a man who declared in 'Why I Write' that his aim was 'to make political writing an art', but the evidence lies strewn around the foothills of his early career. In autumn 1931, for example, shortly after his hop-picking journey to Kent, he can be found writing to Eleanor Jaques from an address in London W9. British political life was at this point descending into turmoil: Ramsay MacDonald's Labour administration was about to be replaced by a National Government. Orwell was alert to the seriousness of the outlook and its consequences for ordinary people – 'There is going to be rioting in London this winter by the looks of things. The dole is cut, money is depreciating in value' – and notes that even in the Bermondsey lodging houses where he had been spending part of his time, labouring men were talking about the 'Bloody Sunday' disturbances of 1888 (in fact these took place in November 1887) when marchers protesting in London about unemployment and coercion in Ireland clashed with police. But his concluding remarks are almost pointedly detached: 'I don't understand or take any interest in the political situation, but evidently all parties are conspiring to keep the left-wing out.'

This analysis of the political manoeuvrings that preceded the general election of October 1931 is correct – MacDonald's Tory-dominated coalition won all but sixty-one seats in the House of Commons – but Orwell himself seems unmoved. There is no reference to it anywhere in his writings from the rest of 1931, or indeed to politics generally. Look for any kind of formal engagement with the political process in the three novels that he published between 1934 and 1936 and there is not much more than a hole in the air. Such mentions as there are of politics are brought in merely to add something to our understanding of the characters or the milieu in which they operate. And so, watching the Tory candidate Mr Blifil-Gordon's election cortège proceeding along Knype Hill high street in *A Clergyman's Daughter*, a disgusted Mr Warburton demands of Dorothy, 'Is there a Socialist candidate? If so, I shall certainly vote for him.' But Mr Warburton has no real interest in politics: he is simply trying to *épater les bourgeois*. The remark has the desired effect, and Mr Twiss, the town's ironmonger, looks on disapprovingly: 'He had caught the word Socialist, and was mentally registering Mr Warburton as a Socialist and Dorothy as the friend of Socialists.'

It is the same with Gordon's arguments with Ravelston in *Keep the Aspidistra Flying*, which are a route into his obstreperousness and general discontent rather than a sign of political awakening. When Ravelston counsels him to read Marx, Gordon ripostes with 'I'd sooner read Mrs Humphry Ward.' Asked to state his objections to socialism, he replies that he has only one – 'Nobody wants it.' Asked what he thinks socialism would mean in practice, he produces a paragraph's worth of scornful invective: 'Oh! Some kind of Aldous Huxley *Brave New World*; only not as amusing. Four hours a day in a model factory, tightening up bolt number 6003. Rations served out in greaseproof paper at the communal kitchen. Community-hikes from Marx Hostel to Lenin Hostel and back. Free abortion-clinics on all the corners. All very well in its way, of course. Only we don't want it.'

As for what we do want, Gordon can only come up with two provocative alternatives: these are suicide and the Catholic Church. Reeling from this assault, Ravelston returns to his flat to be chided by the faithful Hermione on the grounds that his political beliefs are only an invitation to exploit his generosity. The waifs and strays whom he has assembled around him at *Antichrist* are, according to this analysis, there 'to cadge from you'. Of course, she knows that he is a socialist, Hermione continues: 'So am I. I mean we're all Socialists nowadays. But I don't see why you have to give away all your money and make friends with the lower classes. You can be a Socialist *and* have a good time. That's what I say.'

Looking back on his early life, Orwell was always keen to set some of this public indifference in context, claiming for example that he was always inclined towards the left and that he had begun to distrust the influence of the Soviet Union from the early 1930s onwards. A letter from 1945 to a former flatmate whom he suspected of being a communist insists that 'I am against all dictatorships and I think the Russian myth has done frightful harm to the leftwing movement in Britain and elsewhere . . . But I thought all this as early as 1932 or thereabouts and always said so fairly freely.' It is undoubtedly true that much of his early work shows a fair amount of political awareness – 'A Farthing Newspaper', his very first appearance in print in the UK in 1928, is, among other things, an attack on capitalist media barons, and *A Clergyman's Daughter* is keenly alert to 'the mysterious power of money'. On the other hand, little of this engagement was apparent to the people with whom he socialised in London at the time. Sir Richard Rees, the model for Ravelston, marked him down as a 'Bohemian Tory', led into his researches by a straightforward sympathy with the plight of the dispossessed rather than any deep-rooted ideological conviction. Kay Ekevall, who knew him during the early part of his time as a bookseller's assistant, recalled that at no point in their wanderings around Hampstead did he so much as mention politics. Orwell's own account of the Bank Holiday weekend of early May 1935 confirms this sense of detachment. On the Saturday afternoon, short of cash and having forgotten that the banks would not reopen until Tuesday, he called at Rees's flat in search of a loan, only to discover that his friend 'was at some sort of Socialist meeting, and he asked me in and I spent three hours with seven or eight Socialists haranguing me, including a South Wales miner who told me – quite good naturedly, however – that if he were dictator he would have me shot immediately'.

Clearly the Orwell who wrote this knew very little of socialists or socialism. And yet Orwell's social circle during his early years in London was full of people for whom left-wing politics was a matter of the most pressing importance. Ravelston is said to have been trying to convert Gordon to socialism 'for years'. It is highly probable that Rees did the same with Orwell. One of his Hampstead landlords, Francis Westrope, was a leading light in the Independent Labour Party; so was his friend the writer Sam McKechnie. However resistant Orwell may have been to some of the left-wing blandishments on offer, he would have been exposed to them at practically every social event he attended. Sadly Orwell's voting record in the 1920s and 1930s is beyond reconstituting. He was eligible to vote in five electoral contests – the general elections of 1924, 1929, 1931 and 1935, and, given that he was almost certainly on the electoral register of his parents' constituency, the Suffolk division of Lowestoft, the by-election of February 1934 memorialised in *A Clergyman's Daughter* – but in none of them is there the faintest hint of how, or even if, he voted. The 1924 election took place when he was in Burma; the 1929 election when he was in Paris. We can infer that in 1934 he voted Labour owing to his dislike of the Conservative candidate, Pierse Loftus. Did he, like most people of his age and social class, support a National Government candidate in 1931 or 1935? He may well have done in 1931: *The Lion and the*

Unicorn's verdict on that election is that 'we all did the wrong thing in perfect unison'. Beyond that, nothing.

◎

Between 1936 and 1939 the pace of Orwell's life quickens up. In place of adventures among the dispossessed and private school-teaching come war, foreign travel and serious illness. He spent the early part of 1936 in the north of England, collecting material for what would become *The Road to Wigan Pier* (1937). Relocating to the tiny village of Wallington in Hertfordshire, with Eileen, whom he married in early June, he occupied himself in finishing his book before, at the very end of the year, travelling to Barcelona to enlist for the Republican forces in their fight against Franco. Here, in the spring of 1937, he narrowly survived being shot through the throat by a fascist sniper – the bullet missed his carotid artery by a few millimetres. Returning to England he immediately began work on an account of his Spanish experiences, *Homage to Catalonia* (1938). Shortly after the book was completed he was taken ill with what was officially diagnosed as bronchiectasis, despite the evidence of tubercular lesions in his lungs. During the autumn of 1938 and the spring of 1939 he convalesced in Morocco – the funds were supplied by an anonymous well-wisher, later revealed as the novelist L.H. Myers – and worked on his fourth novel, *Coming Up for Air* (1939), which was published a few months before the outbreak of the Second World War.

Inevitably, all these experiences had a profound impact on Orwell's writing. The man who came downstairs on a morning in late August 1939 to read news of the Nazi–Soviet pact was a radically different proposition to the man who, less than three years before, had accepted a £50 advance from Victor Gollancz to investigate social conditions in the Depression-ravaged north of England: politicised, circumspect, thoroughly attuned to the ebb and flow of international power politics. Even so, the process that in 1938 culminated in his decision to join the Independent Labour Party (ILP) and commit himself to the left was far from clear-cut. If the journey that produced *The Road to Wigan Pier* – which appeared in the orange covers of Gollancz's Left Book Club – is sometimes seen as his first decisive political act, then a close inspection of the circumstances in which the book was written tells a rather different story. The Left Book Club selection came late in the day: at the time Orwell left London for the north, the club barely existed; the first advertisements appeared almost a month after he had set out. Neither did Gollancz yet know what he had commissioned: as late as October 1936 he could be found writing to Orwell's agent Leonard Moore to enquire just what exactly the latter's client was up to. Orwell, too, seems to have gone round the north without much of an idea of the uses to which the material collected there might be put. He had assembled 'reams of notes and statistics', he told Richard Rees about halfway through the journey, 'though in what way I shall use them I haven't made up my mind yet'.

And then there is the evidence of the diary entries filed along the way. To watch Orwell at work among the miners and Labour Party activists of Wigan, Barnsley and Sheffield is an odd experience. Keenly observant, highly sympathetic, genuinely shocked by the levels of deprivation and poor housing on display, he approaches the political arrangements of the industrial north with a kind of wide-eyed ingenuousness. Thus, lodging with a man named Meade at the start of his tour in early February, he notes that his host is 'some kind of Trade Union official'. Meade then despatches him to Wigan to see a man named Joe Kennan, represented as 'an electrician who takes a prominent part in the Socialist movement'. What does a trade union official do? What does the 'Socialist movement' consist of? The suspicion is that at this point in his travels, Orwell hasn't much idea. The same kind of mild bewilderment attends his account of a National Unemployed Workers' Union benefit for Ernst Thälmann, the imprisoned German communist. Not impressed by the docility of the audience, he supposes that 'these people represent a fair cross-section of the more revolutionary element in Wigan. If so, God help us.'

The sense that Orwell is feeling his way into the politics of the mid-1930s and arriving at judgements that are instinctive rather than based on ulterior knowledge looms even larger when he arrives in Liverpool. The discovery that the city's rehousing schemes are the brainchild of its Tory corporation, but that the work is largely carried out by private contractors, is the prompt for some rather naïve remarks about the apparent confluence of right and left: 'Beyond a certain point, therefore, Socialism and Capitalism are not easy to distinguish, the State and the Capitalist tending to merge into one.' Significantly, some of his sharpest comments are reserved for class divides and the chasm stretching out between working-class and middle-class lifestyles. Staying with his elder sister Marjorie and her husband in Leeds, for example, he is immediately 'Conscious all the while of the difference in atmosphere between middle-class homes even of this kind and working-class homes.' The Dakin household may have five adults and three children squeezed into its relatively cramped interior, but 'the essential difference is that here there is elbow-room'.

All this leads him into an analysis of the psychology of working-class life: the endless 'waiting about' of the wage-slave compelled to fetch his weekly earnings from his employer in his own time rather than have them paid into his bank account; the serial humiliations of having to deal with supercilious bureaucrats. At one point, staying in Sheffield, he proposes to visit the city hall in search of statistical information. The two working-class men who have undertaken to show him round instantly turn 'nervous' and decline to accompany into the building on the grounds that the official in charge will be obstructive. 'He might give it to *you*, but he wouldn't give it to *us*.' In the event, the man in whose gift the relevant data lies is 'snooty and unforthcoming', but Orwell is suddenly aware of the assumption on which his entry into the room was based: 'the point was that I assumed my questions would be answered, and the other two assumed the contrary.' Then, at a meeting of the South Yorkshire branch of the Working Men's Club and Institute Union, his gaze moves upwards to take in the status anxiety of the more prosperous elements of the working class. If the discontented middle classes were liable to sympathise with fascism, then Orwell could foresee a time when better-off manual workers 'will be mobilised for anti-socialist purposes'.

The Road to Wigan Pier, published in the spring of 1937, was a controversial book, praised for the faithfulness of its reportage – the haunting descriptions of life in the Brookers' lodging house, the account of Orwell's descent to the coalface – but disparaged for both the partiality of its view of conditions in the industrial north and the naïvety of its polemical second half. As for the narrowness of Orwell's gaze, a journalist who had lived in Wigan for years complained that 'He attacked the class barrier at its thickest and highest point. He tried to get into the manual working-class and into a very special section of it – the miners. He chose, moreover, a sub-section of the miners – those out of work; and he chose a sub-section of the unemployed: those who lived in the worst slums.'

Unsurprisingly, there are points to be made in Orwell's favour: one of them is that male unemployment in Wigan in the mid-1930s was estimated to be between a quarter and a third of the adult population. But there is no getting away from the fixity of the lens. Football, dog-racing, variety halls, brass band concerts – hardly anywhere in *The Road to Wigan Pier* is there mention of working-class leisure pursuits or the manifold ways in which ordinary people kept themselves entertained, even at times of intense economic pressure. Meanwhile, the remarks about socialism so antagonised Victor Gollancz that he contributed a foreword to the Left Book Club edition claiming to have 'marked well over a hundred minor passages about which I thought I should like to argue with Mr Orwell'. What was Gollancz complaining about? His principal target seems to be the blanket generalising that Orwell brings to his assaults on 'the typical Socialist'. To Orwell this exemplar is 'Either a youthful snob-

Bolshevik who in five years' time will quite probably have made a wealthy marriage and been converted to Roman Catholicism; or, still more typically, a prim little man with a white-collar job, usually a secret teetotaller and often with vegetarian leanings with a suspicion of nonconformity behind him, and, above all, with a social position which he has no intention of forfeiting.'

This kind of thing caused huge offence in 1937, not merely for its whiff of snobbery – what, after all, is inherently wrong about being a Catholic, a teetotaller, a vegetarian, a non-conformist or even wanting a social position? – but for the suspicion that Orwell, in condemning middle-class socialists for their pretentiousness and crankiness, is silently evading one or two questions about his own relationship to the socialist movement. The second half of *The Road to Wigan Pier* contains a famous passage in which Orwell amuses himself with the memory of a couple of 'dreadful old men' glimpsed on a bus in Letchworth, Hertfordshire, a few miles from his Wallington home:

> They were both about sixty, both very short, pink and chubby, and both hatless. One of them was obscenely bald, the other had long grey hair bobbed in the Lloyd George style. They were dressed in pistachio-coloured shirts and khaki shorts into which their huge bottoms were crammed so tightly that you could study every dimple. Their appearance created a mild stir of horror on top of the bus. The man next to me, a commercial traveller I should say, glanced at me, at them, and back again at me, and murmured 'Socialists', as one who should say, 'Red Indians'. He was probably right – the ILP were holding their summer school at Letchworth. But the point is to him, as an ordinary man, a crank meant a Socialist and a Socialist meant a crank.

Again, Orwell's objections to his fellow-travellers are merely snobbish. The failings for which he is convicting them are arbitrary: lack of height, going hatless, being bald, having fat bottoms, wearing oddly coloured shirts. One might as well criticise Orwell for being six foot three and sporting a toothbrush moustache. Even more important than this, perhaps, is the question of what Orwell was doing on the bus travelling through Letchworth that summer's day in 1936. Enquiry reveals that he, too, was on his way to attend the Independent Labour Party's summer school, whose programme records that he spoke about his experiences in the north. Strictly speaking, the author of *The Road to Wigan Pier* and the two 'dreadful old men' were comrades in arms.

◎

By the time *The Road to Wigan Pier* appeared in the bookshops its author was far away from homegrown socialist cranks and in a place where an attachment to left-wing political causes was a matter of life and death. What sent Orwell to Spain in the last days of 1936 to fight against the Nationalist forces of General Francisco Franco? Several of the people he talked to in the weeks before his departure thought that the decision had a romantic element. He is supposed to have told one friend that if everyone who went to Spain killed a fascist there wouldn't be so many of them left. Philip Mairet, editor of the *New English Weekly*, remembered him remarking, almost like the hero of a boys' school story, that 'something had to be done'. Clearly there were professional reasons for wanting to travel to Barcelona – Orwell admits in the opening pages of *Homage to Catalonia* (1938) that he had 'come to Spain with some notion of writing newspaper articles' – but these were rapidly overtaken by a compulsion to fight. The ILP stalwart Fenner Brockway, who later became a Labour MP, recalled Orwell telling him that while the experience would probably result in a book, 'his idea was to take part in the struggle against Fascism'. Orwell himself notes that he joined the militia on his arrival 'because at that time and in that atmosphere it seemed the only conceivable thing to do'.

The reference to the 'atmosphere' prevailing in Barcelona in the early part of 1937 is significant. Spain, it is safe to say, politicised

Orwell in a way that his exposure to homegrown socialism in the previous five years had not. To begin with, it offered him a vision of how an alternative world, founded on the principles of freedom and equality, might work. And yet, only a few months later, it supplied a chilling example of the perversion of that ideal and its slide into autocracy. The vision came in revolutionary Barcelona, from which Orwell was able to report to Cyril Connolly that he had seen 'wonderful things'. It was, he declared, 'the first time that I had ever been in a town where the working class was in the saddle'. Churches were being systematically demolished by gangs of workmen. Shops and cafes bore inscriptions saying that they had been collectivised. Tipping was forbidden by law, all private motor cars had been commandeered, and all the trams and taxis had been painted in the anarchist colours of red and black. 'In outward appearance it was a town in which the wealthy classes had practically ceased to exist.'

Orwell would later admit that his view of the Spanish Revolution was naïve. At the time he believed that 'things were as they appeared, that this was really a workers' State, and that the entire bourgeoisie had either fled, been killed, or voluntarily come over to the workers' side'. A similar naïvety attended his arrival in Barcelona and some of his subsequent manoeuvrings. He had first intended to join the Soviet-dominated International Marxist Brigade (IMB). Yet the ILP, under whose auspices he had arrived in Spain, was closely connected with the POUM militia, a Trotskyist-cum-anarchist splinter group held in great disfavour by the communist left. Four months later, frustrated by the lack of activity on the Huesca Front – the days of wasted time are recorded in pitiless detail in *Homage to Catalonia* – Orwell, scheming for a transfer to the IMB, at a time when Soviet agents were bent on extirpating rogue elements in the Republican alliance, seems not to have realised that such a move could have had fatal consequences: 'They won't take you,' one of his POUM comrades advised. 'But if they do, they'll knock you off.' Returning to Barcelona after recuperating from his bullet wound,

Orwell discovered that his life was in danger from marauding hit squads. Escaping over the French border with Eileen, who had been in Spain since the early spring working for the ILP, he found that both their names figured on a hit list.

What effect did six months in Spain have on Orwell and his writing? In professional terms the conflict dominated his life for the next two years: much of his journalism between mid-1937 and early 1939 involved 'Spilling the Spanish Beans' (the title of a famous essay), reviewing books about the war and taking part in the numerous controversies that it spawned. Politically, it provided a view of the international stage that could sometimes seem to relegate other actors to a supporting role. As his friend Tosco Fyvel once put it, 'it was his own Spanish experience which shaped his thinking'. Hitler, Mussolini, appeasement, the move towards European war – all these were important, but the tools Orwell used to dissect them had each been acquired in Spain. None of them were more important than his understanding of the uses – and misuses – to which propaganda could be put. It was in Spain that he read newspaper reports of battles that had not taken place or saw soldiers whom he knew to have fought bravely denounced for cowardice. All of this would be channelled into the landscapes of *Nineteen Eighty-Four*.

And it was the experience of fighting in Spain that spurred Orwell towards political activism. The ILP, which he joined in mid-1938, was, he explained to readers of the *New Leader*, the only party 'which aims at anything I should regard as Socialism'. This did not mean that he had taken against the Labour Party, only that he regarded the ILP as 'the only party which . . . is liable to take the right line either against imperialist war or against Fascism when this appears in British form'. What did Orwell regard as socialism? In fact, his work in the period after he joined the ILP is notably light on practical initiatives. He was not, it should immediately be said, a romantic socialist: equality and fraternity were only desirable if they came with higher wages and better living conditions. 'How right the working classes are in their "materialism",' he later wrote. 'How right they are to realize that the belly comes before the soul.' *The Lion and the Unicorn* (1941) offers a six-point programme, advertised as 'the kind of thing we need', including large-scale nationalisation, limitation of incomes, 'reform of the educational system along democratic lines', Dominion status for India, an imperial general council 'in which the coloured peoples are to be represented', and a 'formal alliance' with victims of the fascist powers.

This was a great deal more radical than official Labour Party policy in the early 1940s, and there are one or two later indications that Orwell would have liked to go beyond it. In a contribution to a *Horizon* symposium on 'The Cost of Letters' from September 1946, which posed the question 'How much does a writer need to live on?', he maintained that ideally he would 'like to see every human being have the same income; but so long as there is to be differentiation, I think the writer's place is in the middle bracket, which means, at present standards, round about £1,000 a year'. By and large, his radical inclinations were tempered by an awareness of practical realities – a long article for a German magazine in 1948 about the achievements of the Attlee government accepts that much of its reforming zeal had been frustrated by the unavoidable austerities of the post-war era – and also by the tug of heritage. Having become the proud father of an adopted son in the summer of 1944, the advocate of 'reform of the educational system along democratic lines' told a friend that he intended to put Richard down for Eton.

Here in 1938, with the shadow of war looming ever closer, Orwell's radicalism also extended to pacifism. At this stage he believed that any armed conflict in continental Europe would be a capitalist war fought between adversaries who, however politically separable, were espousing slightly different versions of the same economic principle. According to this argument, the true progressive should only be fighting for international socialism; anything else would simply be shoring up the interests of contending capitalist states. 'Anyone who helps put peace on the map is doing useful work,' he declared in a letter to the *New English Weekly* from May 1938, adding that the real enemies of the working class are those who 'try to trick them into identifying their real interests with those of their exploiters, and forgetting what every manual worker knows – that modern war is a racket'. A letter to Eleanor Jaques, written shortly after he came back from Spain, mentions 'the war which is presumably coming and in which I do not intend to fight'.

All this offers a context for *Coming Up for Air*, the novel on which Orwell worked during his stay in Morocco and whose composition proceeded alongside letters to his anarchist friend Herbert Read advocating direct anti-war action ('I believe it is vitally necessary for those of us who oppose the coming war to start organising for illegal anti-war activities … If we don't make preparations we may find ourselves silenced and absolutely helpless when either war or the pre-war fascising process begins'). George Bowling may be a middle-aged, middle-class everyman bent on revisiting the scenes of his Oxfordshire childhood before the bombs blow them away, but beneath his desultory progress around past and present life lies a series of carefully worked political interventions whose effect is all the more pointed for being focused as much on George's formative years as his ground-down pre-war maturity. Bowling is not perhaps a political animal, but politics is all around him, shaping his life and waiting, or so we infer, to drag him down.

The political arrangements of his childhood in Lower Binfield are hedged around with cynicism, notably in the attitude of the local people to central government. 'They were all true-blue Englishmen and swore that Vicky [Queen Victoria] was the best queen that ever lived and foreigners were dirt,' Bowling recalls, 'but at the same time nobody ever thought of paying a tax, not even a dog-licence, if there was any way of dodging it'. This, we are constantly reminded, is an imperial age, the era of the Boer War – one of his earliest memories is the excitement provoked by the relief of Mafeking – and the source of an enduring row between Bowling's father Samuel and his half-brother Ezekiel. Uncle Ezekiel is a 'Little Englander' fond of denouncing such pro-imperial politicians as Joseph Chamberlain, secretary of state for the colonies between 1895 and 1903, and his allies: 'Them and their far-flung Empire! Can't fling it too far for me.' Bowling remembers his father disagreeing, 'coming back at him with the white man's burden and our dooty to the pore blacks whom these here Boars treated something shameful', but there is a suspicion that Uncle Ezekiel, much more forceful than his milk-and-water sibling, is getting the best of the argument.

Bowling himself is represented as conventionally patriotic, joining up shortly after war is declared in August 1914 on a wave of communal enthusiasm with little thought of what the step entails, only to be disgusted by the horrors of Flanders and shrewdly aware of some of the social processes that it sets in train: by the time the war ends he is a second lieutenant and as such is encouraged to think that he belongs to a superior social class. Yet the novel's two most significant scenes (significant, that is, in terms of Orwell's future development as a writer), coming in quick succession and loaded with symbolic freight, take place in 1938. Each seems faintly incongruous in the light of what we know about Bowling; equally, both are vital to the book's underlying themes. The first finds him attending a meeting of the Left Book Club, here represented as one of the few interests he has in common with his joyless wife. According to Bowling, Hilda 'can see the sense of buying a book when you're getting it for a third of its proper price'. And yet Hilda's presence at Book Club meetings, together with her friends Mrs Wheeler and Miss Minns, is deeply unconvincing: 'Miss Minns certainly had a try at reading one or two of the books, but this wouldn't even have occurred to the other two. They've never had connexion with the Left Book Club or any notion what it's all about – in fact I believe at the beginning Mrs Wheeler thought it had something to do with books which had been left in railway carriages and were being sold off cheap.'

But her husband's arrival at a meeting of the West Bletchley branch addressed by 'Mr so-and-so, the well-known anti-fascist' turns out to be the moment when, politically speaking, *Coming Up for Air* catches flame. Watching the lecturer, of whom he initially approves ('of course he was a good speaker . . . pitching into Hitler and the Nazis'), Bowling eventually concedes that the man is 'working up hate' and that what he is hearing is 'just like a gramophone' blaring out stock phrases ('Bestial atrocities . . . Hideous outbursts of sadism . . . Rubber truncheons'). If this seems uncannily prophetic of the world of *Nineteen Eighty-Four*, with its Two Minutes Hates and Big Brother's Orders of the Day, then it also anticipates the essay 'Politics and the English Language' (1946), which complains about the 'tired hack on the platform mechanically repeating the familiar phrases – *bestial atrocities, iron heel, bloodstained tyranny*'. Then, as Bowling broods over the frightening visions that the lecturer's harangue has called up, comes a direct prefiguration of the landscapes of Airstrip One:

> The coloured shirts, the barbed wire, the rubber truncheons. The secret cells where the electric light burns night and day, and the detectives watching you while you sleep. And the processions and the posters with enormous faces, and the crowds of a million people all cheering for the Leader till they deafen themselves into thinking that they really worship him, and all the time, underneath, they hate him so that they want to puke. It's all going to happen. Or isn't it?

But the Left Book Club meeting is not simply a means for Orwell to rehearse some of the material that will eventually take formal shape in *Nineteen Eighty-Four*; it also offers a chance for Bowling to declare his – and his creator's – pacifism. Asked by a young man if he would fight in a war that offered the chance to 'smash Fascism' once and for all, Bowling shakes his head: 'You bet I wouldn't.' He goes on to explain that his questioner has 'got it all wrong. In 1914 we thought it was going to be a glorious business. Well, it wasn't. It was just a bloody mess. If it comes again, you keep out of it.'

The second scene, which takes place half an hour later, is more prophetic still. Leaving the meeting, Bowling decides to drop in on a friend of his, a retired public school classics master named Porteous, a man who lives his life in a state of almost complete detachment from the modern world. What is Porteous, whose presence in Bowling's life is never explained – he is simply 'a pal of mine' – doing in the novel? Like the Left Book Club lecture, he is there to provide Bowling (and Orwell) with an opportunity to pronounce on the nature of contemporary despotism. Informed by Porteous that tyrants such as Hitler and Stalin are 'purely ephemeral' and matched in their depravity by some of the rulers of the ancient world, Bowling disagrees. Porteous is wrong about the modern-day dictators: 'They aren't like these chaps in the old days who crucified people and chopped their heads off, just for fun. They're after something quite new – something that's never been heard of before.' And then comes another twitch on the thread that simultaneously takes us back to Gordon Comstock's laments about his poems and forward to Winston Smith: 'He's dead,' Bowling decides, as Porteous starts reading 'Ode to a Nightingale' to him. 'He's a ghost. All people like that are dead.'

Having failed to convince his friend that 'Hitler matters', Bowling walks home turning over in his mind his worries about the international situation and the mundane irritations of his domestic life: 'At that moment the destiny of Europe seemed to me more important than the rent and the kids' school-bills and the work I'd have to do tomorrow.' All the same, his final thought before falling asleep is 'why the hell a chap like me should care'. *Coming Up for Air* was published in June 1939, three months before the Second World War broke out. By September, Orwell's views had undergone a decisive shift. Staying with L.H. Myers in Hampshire late in August, he found himself dreaming that the war had already broken out; not only this, but there was relief in putting an end to months of uncertainty, accompanied by a conviction that at heart he was a patriot who would support the war. Waking up, he stumbled downstairs to be greeted by newspaper headlines announcing the Hitler–Stalin pact. Within a fortnight he would be writing to the authorities in search of war work.

If *Coming Up for Air* is in some sense a memento of Orwell's political journey between 1936 and 1939, then it also offers a hint of where that voyage would take him in the next few years. 'They think that England will never change and that England's the whole world,' Bowling observes about people like Porteous. Much of Orwell's writing in the early years of the war would define him as a radical nationalist, a patriotic Englishman thoroughly dissatisfied with the country of his birth and bent on reimagining it to meet some of the challenges of the modern age.

Taking part in the BBC North American Service's Answering You, *October 1942.*

6

STYLE

'POLITICS AND THE ENGLISH LANGUAGE' • 'MARRAKECH'

Orwell's work is full of prescriptive remarks on how books should and shouldn't be written. 'Good prose is like a windowpane.' 'For my part I like a florid style'. 'Inside the Whale' (1940) praises Henry Miller for bringing back the adjective 'after its ten years' exile' and commends his 'flowing, swelling prose, a prose with rhythms in it, something quite different from the flat cautious statements and snack-bar dialects that are now in fashion'. There are also several withering take-downs of the double negative, and the occasional assault on punctuation: he once claimed that *Coming Up for Air* purposely excludes all use of the semi-colon. Yet the most considerable statement of his views on what makes 'good writing' can be found in 'Politics and the English Language', originally intended for George (later Lord) Weidenfeld's magazine *Contact* but eventually published in *Horizon* in the spring of 1946. Here he sets down six general principles for the aspiring prose stylist: never use a metaphor, simile or other figure of speech if its use is already commonplace; never use a long word where a short one will do; if you can cut out a word then do so; use the active tense rather than the passive; never use a foreign phrase, a scientific expression or a piece of jargon if you can find an everyday English equivalent; finally, break any of these rules sooner than say anything 'outright barbarous'.

If closely pressed, Orwell would probably have agreed that much of this advice is both contradictory and overstated. Take, for example, that famous claim that 'Good prose is like a windowpane'. One can think of several varieties of prose, some of them admired by Orwell – Joyce's *Ulysses*, for instance – that aren't in the least transparent and take a positive pride in declining to yield up their intent. Then there is that prejudice against the double negative, which however clumsy it may look on the printed page introduces an element of nuance into a judgement whose deciphering can produce something tantalisingly ambiguous. After all, when a critic describes a book as 'not wholly unsuccessful', they are essentially setting up a judgemental puzzle for the reader to solve. How unsuccessful is 'not wholly unsuccessful'? Does the critic approve or disapprove, and if so to what extent? And what do we mean by 'success'? Seen in this light, a blizzard of qualification and the absence of anything definite may actually work to the readers' advantage, prompting them to think harder about the book in question rather than accepting a reductive verdict of 'good' or 'bad'.

It should also be pointed out that Orwell often breaks his own rules – see, for example, at any rate at the start of his career, his fondness for classical tags and French phrases picked up at school. And yet, in the end, these transgressions are irrelevant, for Orwell's style is one of the greatest things about him – sharp, direct, transfixing, instantly reducing the barrier that sometimes exists between even the most well-meaning writer and their audience to a pile of fragments. At bottom this has something to do with sheer *emphasis*. The most casual observer of Orwell's work will usually be struck by its assertiveness, its impenitent self-confidence, his habit of using the adjectives first heard in Edwardian drawing rooms – 'beastly' (a word he is first recorded as having uttered as a child of eighteen months), 'monstrous', 'vile', 'awful', 'frightful', 'dreadful' – in settings where something much less hyperbolic would do. But Orwell's characters have 'monstrous faces', they are 'beastly cold', and sit at desks surrounded by 'frightful jumbles of paper', and the world they inhabit is characterised by a kind of Brobdingnagian heightening of emotion and detail. Even when setting the scene for 'Boys' Weeklies' (1940), the newsagents' shops where copies of *Magnet* and *Gem* can be found are said to consist of 'a dark interior smelling of liquorice allsorts and festooned from floor to ceiling with vilely printed twopenny papers'. Certainly, the magazines are brightly coloured and cheaply produced, but *vile*, whose *Shorter Oxford* definition is 'despicable on moral grounds'? Brought to Orwell's professional beat or the landscapes of international power politics, this combination of plain speaking and hypertrophy can bring off devastating effects: 'kissing the bums of verminous little lions' (of book reviewing); 'all the smelly little ortho-doxies that are now contending for our souls' (the state of the world in 1939). V.S. Pritchett once singled out a paragraph of Orwell's writing that began with the words, 'It is a strange fact, but it is unquestionably true that almost any English intellectual would feel more ashamed of standing to attention during "God Save the King" than of stealing from a poor box.' The statement itself can be marked down as all too questionable: what Pritchett (and most readers who came after him) liked was the self-assurance of the tone.

In all of this there lurks a suspicion of stage-management, aesthetic sleight of hand. One of Orwell's most characteristic literary tricks is his habit of twisting words out of their usual shape and giving them a significance that they wouldn't usually possess. 'Monstrous' is a favourite here, but also 'debauched' and 'loathly'. And so in *Burmese Days* Flory walks outside to be greeted by a 'debauch of sun'. U Po Kyin's daily blow-outs at the dinner table are described as 'debauches of curry and rice'. Certainly the temperature is in the eighties and the Burmese magistrate is over-eating, but does either of these things really constitute a 'debauch'? But the tendency goes back to Orwell's very earliest writings. In 'The Spike', for example, he records one of the tramps with whom he has spent the night in a casual ward returning a favour by presenting him with 'four sodden, debauched, loathly cigarette ends'. It is the same in *The Road to Wigan Pier* when, far underground on one of his visits to a coal mine, Orwell puts out his hand into the darkness and finds 'a dreadful slimy thing' among the coal dust. This turns out to be a quid of chewed tobacco – not a pleasant object to come across, perhaps, but Orwell makes it sound like an unimaginable horror, a phantom from an M.R. James ghost story come to haunt him from the shadows.

But *The Road to Wigan Pier* is a kind of masterclass in what might be called the pejoratively emotive, in which the writer can be seen hard at work accentuating the negative by way of devious use of language. One might note Orwell's unflagging pursuit of the Brookers, the unprepossessing couple who run the lodging house in which he stays. It is clear from an early stage in Orwell's description of the premises that any ammunition will do, that he dislikes his hosts and their squalid way of life so much that any foibles they possess will be fuel for the flame. It is not just that the carpet is 'ringed with the slop-pails of years', but that neither the landlord nor his wife has a chance when set against the sharp-eyed southerner who complains of Mr Brooker peeling potatoes into a 'tub of filthy water' – as if any water into which potatoes were peeled could ever be clean. From here it is only a short step to the 'dark subterranean place' – that is, a basement – in which the tripe is stored. Even the food – Orwell is encouraged to eat 'pale flabby Lancashire cheese' – turns out to be morally suspect.

None of this matters in the slightest, of course. Such is the vigour of the prose and the eye for detail – as when Orwell claims that the dining table was so rarely swept that he got to know individual crumbs by sight and was able to track their progress around the surface – that the reader ceases to care about the Brookers or whether the evidence against them has been manufactured, and simply revels in their exposure. On the other hand, it takes a special kind of confidence to carry these sorts of techniques off.

The same air of self-assurance hangs over the opening lines of nearly every Orwell essay. They tend to be aphoristic and/or evocative, but in almost every case end up by setting the reader a challenge, or pose a question that needs to be answered:

> Dickens is one of those writers who are well worth stealing. Even the burial of his body in Westminster Abbey was a species of theft, if you come to think about it. ('Charles Dickens')

> As I write, highly civilised human beings are flying overhead, trying to kill me. (*The Lion and the Unicorn*)

> The first sound in the mornings was the clumping of the mill-girls' clogs down the cobbled street. Earlier than that, I suppose, there were factory whistles which I was never awake to hear. (*The Road to Wigan Pier*)

All these extracts, in their various ways, are extraordinarily suggestive. Why is Dickens's burial in Westminster Abbey 'a species of theft'? Fifty pages later, the reader will probably conclude that an establishment funeral had the effect of detaching him from the English people and thereby camouflaging the radical strain that runs through his work, but none of this is detectable in the bald statement with which the essay begins. Who are the highly civilised human beings who are flying overhead trying to kill him? (Orwell began work on *The Lion and the Unicorn* in the garden of a Berkshire farmhouse at the height of the Battle of Britain in the summer of 1940.) And then there is the paradox of the highly civilised person who wants to deal out death. If the Wigan extract comes from a slightly different coign of vantage, and deals in situational problems – where is Orwell? Why are the mill-girls clumping down the cobbled streets? – then the spark it sets off in the reader's mind is no less potent. Even Orwell's bread-and-butter journalism has this quality. 'Modern man is rather like a bisected wasp which goes on eating jam and pretending that the loss of its abdomen does not matter,' he asserts at the beginning of a review of Henry Miller's novel *Tropic of Cancer*. Only later – and in a completely separate piece of writing – will the reader discover that modern man resembles the bisected wasp through having parted company with his soul.

The Miller review is a good example of Orwell's eagerness to lay down the law, his habit of making sweeping statements which, in the majority of cases, are there merely to provoke the reader. This is especially true of his novels, which come crammed with what can occasionally seem to be absurd generalisations about human behaviour presented as incontrovertible fact:

> If you want to know what a dead man's relatives think of him, a good rough test is the weight of his tombstone. (*Keep the Aspidistra Flying*)
>
> Every intelligent boy of sixteen is a Socialist. (*The Road to Wigan Pier*)
>
> Most people can be at home in a foreign country only when they are disparaging the inhabitants. (*Burmese Days*)

Nearly every extended piece of Orwell's writing will throw up half a dozen examples of this tendency to dogmatic and highly provocative assertion. When Bowling tries to sum up his delinquent brother Joe in *Coming Up for Air*, we are informed that 'like most half-wits' he had a slight mechanical turn. Discussing the apparent lack of class distinctions on the ship that carries Elizabeth Lackersteen to Burma, *Burmese Days* notes that 'on board ship everyone behaves as though he were rich'. 'No rich man ever succeeds in disguising himself as a poor man' is *Keep the Aspidistra Flying*'s comment on Ravelston's attempts to cross the class divide. Sometimes these assertions are intimately linked to the circumstances of Orwell's own life; knowing what we do of his time spent teaching on the west London private school circuit in the early 1930s, the claim made in *A Clergyman's Daughter* that 'There is perhaps no quarter of the inhabited world where one can be so completely alone as in the London suburbs' sounds peculiarly personal and heartfelt. In nearly all cases, though, these epigrams are horribly suspect. The line about all sixteen-year-old boys being socialists was written in 1936, when Orwell was thirty-three, several years away from school-teaching and living in a remote Hertfordshire village with his first wife. How many sixteen-year-old boys, you wonder, did he know at this time? Again, the fundamental shakiness of these judgements scarcely matters. It is the pose of infallibility that draws the reader in and seduces them. Malcolm Muggeridge has written amusingly about Orwell's famous claim that 'All tobacconists are Fascists'. Nonsense, Muggeridge pronounced, before falling into the trap that Orwell had set him, considering the spectacle of all those irascible middle-aged men peddling their grievances behind a succession of tiny shop-counters and wondering if, in the end, Orwell didn't have a point.

The significance of this habit of generalising lies in its application to character. Although his novels and pieces of reportage are full of sharp, individual portraits, Orwell was fascinated by the idea of 'types', categories of behavioural psychology into which most human life could be neatly slotted. This gives them an odd, Linnean zeal, as if the writer's first aim, when considering one of his characters or someone met along the way, is how much they conform to recognisable patterns of existence – if indeed those patterns are recognisable in the first place. *The Road to Wigan Pier* is full of this kind of *placement*. Mr Brooker, he of the filthy potato-peeling, is 'one of those people who can chew their grievances like a cud'. Additionally, 'like all people with permanently dirty hands he had a peculiarly intimate, lingering way of handling things'. Husband and wife, meanwhile, are characterised as the sort of people who keep a lodging house simply to have something to complain about. When it comes to the individual lodgers, 'Joe', whom Orwell observes with interest, is merely an agglomeration of general characteristics. To begin with, he is 'the kind of person who has no surname'. Elsewhere he is described as 'the typical unmarried unemployed man'. Then, 'like so many unemployed men he spent too much time reading newspapers'.

Invariably, this urge to classify works both ways. On the one hand, the reader may suspect that Orwell's taxonomies are based on insufficient observation, that a few weeks in the north of England may not be long enough to allow anyone to pronounce on the habits of typical unmarried unemployed men or convict them of the fault of reading too many newspapers. On the other, there is also something deeply reassuring about it: the hint of solidarity, community, group behaviour born of custom, class and caste, with Orwell at the centre of it, making his judgements, extending his sympathy or sometimes – rather often in *The Road to Wigan Pier* – withholding it. But the novels strike exactly the same collectivising note. Mr Macgregor, the khaki-shorted district commissioner in *Burmese Days*, is 'like one of those beastly middle-aged scoutmasters, homosexuals almost to a man, that you see photographs of in the illustrated papers'. Turn to *Keep the Aspidistra Flying*, and Mrs Wisbeach, Gordon Comstock's tyrannical landlady, is 'one of those malignant respectable women who keep lodging-houses'. As for Gordon's fellow lodgers, Flaxman possesses 'the typical fat man's good humour' while the reclusive Lorenheim is 'one of those people who have not a single friend in the world and who are devoured by a lust for company'. Even the members of Gordon's family are instantly transformed into 'types'. Julia, his sister, leads 'the typical submerged life of the penniless unmarried woman', while old Grandpa Comstock is 'one of those people who even from the grave exert a powerful influence'. It is the same with Rosemary, who at the moment we first meet her is said to possess 'one of those small, peaky faces, full of character, which one sees in sixteenth-century portraits'.

'The kind of man who . . . The kind of people who . . . In that kind of house . . . One of those huge hungry families . . . Dark and sluttish, as all Burmese rooms are . . .' There are times when the net thrown over Orwell's characters can seem a bit too tightly drawn. By the time of *Coming Up for Air*, hardly anyone seems able to escape it. Joe, Bowling's scapegrace brother, is 'one of those boys who can go through years of schooling and at the end of it are unable to read ten lines consecutively'. Elsie, his first love, is 'one of those girls that always look their best in black'. Bowling, relocated to west London in the years after the Great War, is 'the usual young city worker', while Hilda, whom he marries, is 'one of those people who never say much, but remain on the edge of any conversation that's going on and give the impression that they're listening'. At the same time, Bowling's irresistible urge to classify is wholly understandable and in the end desirable. This, after all, is his novel, which relies for most of its effects on the (sometimes) rough and ready standards he brings to human behaviour. It is the same with the book's jaunty, interrogative style ('Do you know these Anglo-Indian families?' 'Do you ever go to lectures, public meetings and what-not?'), which meets the reader head-on and achieves a kind of complicity of tone. However great the distance between us, Bowling seems to be saying, you and I are in this together.

The stylistic gap between *Coming Up for Air* and its three predecessors declares itself in other ways. Written in the first person, and masquerading as the autobiography of a lower-middle-class insurance representative, it lacks many of the signature marks of Orwell's novels of the early 1930s. Not only are the latter rife with classical tags, some of them relatively abstruse (*anima naturaliter Nonconformistica*, say, or *Ex ecclesiam nulla satis*), they are also dense with literary reference. Most of the literary favourites pressed into service this way are bright particular stars of the English canon – Dickens (a minor Eurasian character in *Burmese Days* is compared to *Martin Chuzzlewit*'s Mr Chollop; in the same novel, Flory wonders if he resembles *Nicholas Nickleby*'s Mrs Wititterley), Milton (several quotations from *Paradise Lost*) and Shakespeare, for example – but it takes only a glance at a novel like *Keep the Aspidistra Flying* to reveal the full extent of Orwell's literary gleanings, a tide of allusion in which there is space for an abundance of French, biblical, classical and English borrowings. Aeschylus, Virgil, Horace, Chaucer, Villon, *The Ingoldsby Legends*, Felicia Hemans and Sir Thomas Wyatt all feature, and an extraordinary passage pastiching the joys of spring makes space for two medieval ballads, Swinburne's 'Hounds of Spring', *As You Like It* and Thomas Nashe's 'Spring, the Sweet Spring'. An annotator once calculated that the novel contains two dozen distinct literary allusions: there are probably more. The set books to which Orwell refers, either by name or implicitly, in his fiction would fill a small library.

◎

How does this work in practice? 'Marrakech', the solitary souvenir of Orwell's time in Morocco, was written sometime in early to mid-1939 and published in the Christmas edition of John Lehmann's *New Writing*. It is a short piece, not more than a few pages long, and consists of five sharply observed vignettes – Orwell monitoring a funeral, feeding stale bread to a gazelle in the municipal park, watching old women carry firewood, wandering in the Jewish quarter and eyeing up a file of Senegalese soldiers – each of which introduces a series of reflections on such topics as colonialism, antisemitism and race relations. There is the usual arresting opening sentence ('As the corpse went past the flies left the restaurant table in a cloud and rushed after it, but they came back a few minutes later') and the customary file of eye-catching generalisations: 'Gazelles are almost the only animals that look good enough to eat when they are still alive ... All people who work with their hands are partly invisible and the more important the work they do, the less visible they are ... In a tropical landscape one's eyes take in everything except the human beings ... It was the shy, wide-eyed negro look, which is actually a look of profound respect.' There is also a bumper helping of Orwell's favourite adjectives and adverbs (the 'frightful labour' needed to cultivate Morocco's barren landscapes, the 'damnable' treatment of the donkey population) and the usual eye for vivid and sometimes uncomfortable detail – the little river of urine that runs down the middle of the Jewish quarter's streets; the carpenter whose leg is warped out of shape by a lifetime's sitting in the same position to work his lathe.

The piece comes to a halt with a description of the black army moving on southwards through the dust: 'And really it was almost like watching a flock of cattle to see the long column, a mile or two miles of armed men, flowing peacefully up the road, while the great white birds drifted over them in the opposite direction, glittering like scraps of paper.' The passage gets its kick from the reflections which have preceded it. Black men in Africa admire their white superiors, Orwell argues. Catching the eye of one of the soldiers, he notes that 'This wretched boy, who is a French citizen and has therefore been dragged from the forest to scrub floors and catch syphilis in garrison towns, actually has feelings of reverence for a white skin. He has been taught that the white race are his masters, and he still believes it.' But how long will it be before they turn their guns in the other direction? All this gives the figurative language of the final sentence a wholly deceptive sheen. The column of men is like 'a flock of cattle' or a river 'flowing peacefully up the road'. Meanwhile, the birds 'drift' over them, 'glittering' as they go. It would seem practically idyllic were it not for the reader's awareness that this is an army and that, here in the early months of 1939, war looms ever closer.

Significantly, much of the figurative language in 'Marrakech' is drawn from the natural world. Lamenting the fact that, as he saw it, impoverished people in North Africa have so few distinguishing features that 'it is difficult to believe that you are walking among human beings', Orwell wonders 'Are they really the same flesh as yourself? Do they even have names? Or are they merely a kind of undifferentiated brown stuff, about as individual as bees or coral insects?' In the Jewish quarter the children cluster 'like clouds of flies'. The Senegalese soldiers are like a cattle herd, lumbering on across the dusty earth. To a modern sensibility all this may look like casual racism. In fact it is just one of Orwell's by now patented stylistic tics – that urge to compare, calibrate and construct endless associative chains around the people and environments in which he was set down, which doesn't by any means ignore some of the power dynamics that lie at their heart. Orwell, it turns out, is never so happy as when comparing something to fauna or flora. Even in the machine-age dystopia that is *Nineteen Eighty-Four* there is still plenty of room for the imagery of the farmyard. O'Brien, for example, when discussing state intervention in family life, talks of taking a child from its mother 'as one takes an egg from a hen'. Yet more striking is the interdependence of the three totalitarian states, Oceania, Eurasia and Eastasia, which are described as leaning on each other to keep themselves upright 'like three stooks in a hayfield'.

This is not to say that Orwell's use of 'nature' for comparative purposes is at all straightforward. It is not enough for Orwell that girls are flower-like; the late-night shoppers on whom Gordon spies in *Keep the Aspidistra Flying* have to resemble a particular kind of flower. But how many of his readers will appreciate the difference between a sweet william and a phlox? Precision is everything, and the stone sent spinning across the ice at Rudyard Lake during the *Road to Wigan Pier* trip makes a noise like a redshank. Later, when Gordon and Rosemary go on an excursion to Burnham Beeches and wander ecstatically through the trees, the figurative lever tugs in the opposite direction, prompting Gordon to remark 'that the little knobs on the bark were like the nipples of breasts and that the sinuous upper boughs, with their smooth, sooty skin, were like the writhing trunks of elephants'.

This is meant to be funny – in the next paragraph Gordon compares the hornbeam foliage to 'the hair of Burne-Jones maidens' – but, again, the exactitude demonstrates just how closely Orwell had looked at nature and how deeply what he saw had penetrated his understanding of language. On the other hand, it is clear that what he really liked doing was comparing people to animals. If the tendency is comparatively subdued in *Burmese Days* – although Mrs Lackersteen, with her 'delicate saurian hands', is clearly first cousin to a lizard – then by the time of *Keep the Aspidistra Flying* it has got completely out of hand. Gordon, dealing with the clientele of Mr McKechnie's bookshop, might as well be working in a menagerie – or perhaps an aviary, given that Mrs Penn, a devotee of the establishment's small circulating library, is described as 'a plump little sparrow of a woman' and that a young man seen poring over a book is 'like some long-legged bird with its head buried under its wing'. Rodents score highly – the hero of the advert for Bovex which Gordon detests so much is 'a bespectacled rat-faced clerk'; the browsing young man holds a book in his hands 'as a squirrel holds a nut' – as do insectivora: the two vagrants who attempt to unload a battered collection of Victorian novels are thought to be 'beetle-like'.

By about halfway through the book the cavalcade of nature imagery has turned into a riot. Modern man, as envisaged by the advertising industry, is 'a docile little porker'. Lorenheim, Gordon's fellow lodger, is 'a dark, meagre, lizard-like creature'. In stark contrast to the browsing young man who steals into Mr McKechnie's shop 'as apologetically as a cat', a woman visiting the Lambeth library at which Gordon eventually fetches up moves 'as clumsily as a bear'. Fear of the sack afflicts the average clerical worker 'like a maggot in his heart'. Interestingly, some of Orwell's liveliest efforts in this line are brought to bear on Rosemary. Walking beside Gordon, after they meet by chance at the evening street market, 'she had the appearance of something extremely small, nimble and young, as though he had some lively little animal, a squirrel for instance, frisking at his side'. But then Gordon, who on the very first page of the novel is described as 'a small, frail figure with delicate bones and fretful movements', has squirrel-like tendencies himself. Clearly the two young people are made for each other.

Pigs, cats, bears, beetles, lizards, squirrels, sparrows – the cast of *Keep the Aspidistra Flying* is a walking bestiary. But Orwell's interest in the natural world goes a good deal further than this. Each of his first four novels contains a purple passage – sometimes there is more than one – in which he temporarily abandons the direct, button-holing style and decides to let himself go on the beauties of nature. In *Burmese Days* the moment comes when Flory takes Elizabeth out hunting in the forest: a dense and well-nigh miraculous tableau in which green pigeons dash towards them 'like a handful of catapulted stones whirling through the sky' and tangled bushes and creepers curl around the tree trunks 'like the sea round the piles of a pier'. In *A Clergyman's Daughter* it arrives when Dorothy, on the way back from anointing Mrs Pither's legs with embrocation, loiters in the summer sunshine, falls to her knees behind a hedge and pulls a frond of fennel against her face: 'Its richness overwhelmed her, almost dazzled her for a moment. She drank it in, filling her lungs with it. Lovely, lovely scent – scent of summer days, scent of summer joys, scent of spice-drenched islands in the warm foam of oriental seas.' Dorothy, of course, has never been anywhere near an oriental sea. Her bathing excursions are confined to the Suffolk coast. This is Orwell remembering his time in Burma.

For Gordon and Rosemary, the nature epiphany materialises on their Sunday excursion to the countryside. Here, on Farnham Common, near Slough, they 'exclaim at the loveliness of everything. The dew, the stillness, the satiny stems of the birches, the softness of the turf under your feet!' Later on they lose themselves among the beech trees, which 'soared, curiously phallic with their smooth skin-like bark and their flutings at the base'. Subsequently the sun comes out and the light 'came slanting and yellow across the fields, and delicate unexpected colours sprang out in everything, as though some giant's child had been let loose with a new paintbox'. Bowling in *Coming Up for Air* is no less susceptible. Stopping his car at the road-side on a spring day next to a patch of primroses, breathing in the

March air and noticing the embers of a fire left by a tramp, he suddenly finds himself renewed: 'What I felt was something that's so unusual nowadays that to say it sounds like foolishness. I felt *happy*.' The scene is instantly undercut by comedy, or at least Bowling's realisation of who he is ('A fat man of forty-five, in a grey herring-bone suit a bit the worse for wear and a bowler hat'), but the effect is undeniable. Bowling's 'red face and boiled blue eyes' – none of this matters when set against the pleasure he is experiencing.

The most conspicuous thing about all four passages is how *un*-Orwellian they seem: in the context of *Keep the Aspidistra Flying*'s end-of-tether rantings about the end of civilisation and the state of English literature, Gordon's adventures in the beech woods are a kind of oasis set amid acres of wind-blown desert. Their significance lies in their connection to the wider pattern of the novels. For Bowling, the primroses are a catalyst. Smelling them, he thinks of his childhood in Lower Binfield and resolves to go back. But in *Burmese Days* and *Keep the Aspidistra Flying*, the purple passages inspired by the natural world have a romantic aspect. Orwell's friend Tosco Fyvel once pointed out that he tended to let himself go when his feelings about nature and his feelings about women ran in parallel. The scenes in which Gordon and Rosemary wander through the woods are rife with sexual imagery (the knobs on the bark that resemble breasts, the 'phallic' look of the trees), while Flory and Elizabeth experience an almost Lawrentian moment out hunting in the Burmese jungle when their hands meet over the corpse of a leopard Flory has just shot; walking back across the stubble fields they are 'happy with that inordinate happiness that comes of exhaustion and achievement, and with which nothing else in life – no joy of either the body or the mind – is even able to be compared'.

From here it is but a short step to the intensely romanticised passages in *Nineteen Eighty-Four* in which Winston and Julia escape to the countryside ('They were standing in the shade of hazel bushes. The sunlight, filtering through innumerable leaves, was still hot on their faces') and Winston's vision of the 'Golden Country' – the idyllic rural bolthole that comes to him in his dreams and is now made real. Once again, the imagery conflates natural and female beauty (the leaves of the elm trees stir 'in dense masses like women's hair'). The significance of Orwell's nature-worship and the way in which it infiltrates his prose style is its connection to his original literary ambitions. The Orwell who generalises about human behaviour and lays down the law about psychological and situational detail – 'Every public school has its small, self-contained intelligentsia'; 'Really vital people, whether they have money or whether they haven't, multiply almost as automatically as animals' – is importing the techniques of journalism into his fiction. The Orwell who writes about beech leaves stirring like women's hair or fat men of forty-five picking primroses in the March sunshine is very close to being an aesthete.

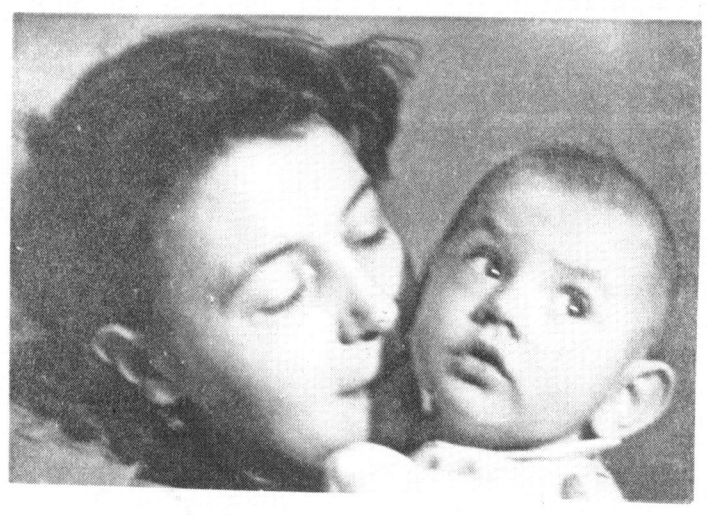

Eileen with Richard, shortly before her death.

7

WOMEN

*BURMESE DAYS • A CLERGYMAN'S DAUGHTER •
KEEP THE ASPIDISTRA FLYING • COMING UP
FOR AIR • THE ROAD TO WIGAN PIER*

What did Orwell think of women? And perhaps more important, what did women think of him? Many of the site reports are not encouraging. He liked women to be interesting and intelligent, a girl who knew him in Hampstead in the mid-1930s remembered, but found it hard to take that they could give back as good as they got. Basil, the character thought to resemble Orwell in Stevie Smith's *The Holiday*, is described as being like 'a fourteen-year-old boy, you know, he thinks girls can't play'. Even more incriminating is the scene in which Basil comes across an article in an American women's magazine advertising a range of underwear known as 'scanty panties'. The long monologue which follows is authentically Orwellian: 'He said women who thought about scanty panties never had a comfortable fire burning in the fire-place, or a baby in the house, or a dog or a cat or a parrot.' Orwell was a domineering character, his old friend Dennis Collings suggested, and as such highly attractive to girls who, unlike his own future wife Eleanor Jaques, were happy to play a subservient role.

According to her daughter, Eleanor turned Orwell down for being either 'too cynical or too sardonic'. Eileen O'Shaughnessy, who did consent to marry him in 1936, seems to have been under no illusions about what she was taking on. Comparing her newly married husband to her adored elder brother Laurence, she remarked that in dire necessity she could summon Laurence from the other side of the world and expect him to arrive. George, on the other hand, would not do this. All the evidence insists that Orwell loved his wife, and she him – her colleagues in the ILP office in Barcelona remembered that she talked about him all the time – but her letters can often find her drowning in tides of self-effacement and humorously expressed resentment. There is a particularly awful one sent from the nursing home on whose operating table she died in the spring of 1945 wondering whether she is worth the money Orwell is having to pay for her surgery. Several of her friends puzzled over her decision to leave unfinished a Birkbeck master's degree in psychology in order to join him in the Wallington cottage. Here was a highly intelligent woman who had given up her independence and her academic prospects to act as nursemaid to a not especially successful writer. What did she think she was doing? To a feminist critic such as Anna Funder, Orwell's treatment of his first wife not only constitutes neglect and belittlement on a grand scale, but amounts to a deliberate erasure of her talents and personality.

Stevie Smith's line about girls 'not playing' is all the more revealing in the context of Orwell's critical work, which betrays an altogether spectacular lack of interest in books by or about women. Dickens, Thackeray, Gissing, Samuel Butler – most of the great male Victorian writers are the subject of individual essays, as well as a volley of supplementary remarks, and yet female contemporaries are conspicuous by their absence. In fact, a trawl through the index to the eleven volumes of the *Complete Works* devoted to his journalism yields up exactly six references to George Eliot, four to Jane Austen and a solitary mention of Charlotte M. Yonge. Orwell's twentieth-century female contemporaries feature a little more strongly – there are approving remarks about Rosamond Lehmann and May Sinclair, and Edith Sitwell's study of Alexander Pope is actually the subject of a whole review – but Katherine Mansfield and Jean Rhys might just as well not have set pen to paper, so reluctant is Orwell to mention them in print.

It is not that Orwell didn't know women writers or that he jibbed at sponsoring their work. There were several female contributors to *Voice*, the literary magazine of the airwaves that he conducted during the latter part of his time at the BBC's Eastern Service, but the women involved – Smith, for example, or Inez Holden – tended to be personal friends, or, in Holden's case, women for whom he had romantic feelings. The young reviewers he encouraged during his time at *Tribune* in 1943–5 were exclusively male. So were most of the literary friends he made in the 1940s. It would be overstating the case to argue that Orwell's professional life in his final decade was a boys' club pure and simple – his collection of highly intelligent female colleagues included the *New Statesman*'s Evelyn Anderson and Celia Kirwan, first found working on *Polemic* before her transfer to the Foreign Office's Information Research Department, and he got on well with the novelist and editor Kay Dick. All the same, most of the women who left reminiscences of him turn out to be the wives of his male friends.

That leaves the nine full-length books. What does Orwell have to say about women in them? Orwell's fiction is full of women – wives, girlfriends, lodging-house keepers, lost loves, bookshop browsers. Few of them are particularly enticing, and those that are (Rosemary, Julia) tend to be women with some kind of tethering in his own emotional life. Of the three women with starring roles in *Burmese Days*, Mrs Lackersteen is a complacent, self-interested snob whose uppermost aims in life are to stop her husband from drinking himself to death and to see her niece safely married; Elizabeth a slightly more amiable younger version of her aunt; and Ma Hla May a duplicitous and (understandably) opportunistic prostitute. Orwell's judgment on Elizabeth is especially revealing, for the portrait of her and the analysis of her motives is in certain respects a rather rounded one. The orphaned daughter of an ineffectual 'artist' and a businessman who loses his money, brought up in the shadow of *luxe* and gentility but never quite able to secure these amenities for herself, sent to a fashionable boarding school and then hastily withdrawn from it when her father's career goes smash, Elizabeth looks as if she deserves our sympathy. At the same time Orwell can never quite forgive her for her shallowness, her snobbery and – worst of all from the angle of the book-starved Flory – her intellectual pretensions. And so she is damned for subscribing to the conventions of a class whose clutches she had no way of escaping in the first place, fated to become the burra memsahib that nature always intended her to be.

A Clergyman's Daughter, too, is chock-full of women: Dorothy, its naïve and put-upon heroine, town gossips and coffee-shop habitués, the private school proprietor Mrs Creevy and even, in the shape of Mrs McElligott, whom Dorothy encounters in the Kentish hop fields, a bona fide female tramp. But Dorothy is a special case – gauche, devout, sympathetic yet transparently a device that Orwell has to insert into the novel to allow all the autobiographical elements of which the book consists to make sense. If anything distinguishes the female supporting cast, it is their futility. Women, Orwell seems to suggest here, are put on earth to worship false gods, to nurture ambitions that are not worth the having, to derive pleasure from backbiting and score-settling or deliberately denying themselves fulfilling lives. Mrs Creevy, the she-dragon of Ringwood House, who declines to celebrate Christmas on the grounds that the festival is 'got up' by shopkeepers, is an early example of one of Orwell's most enduring types – the dyed-in-the-wool female puritan whose hostility to material satisfaction is a kind of sensualism by default. It is a nicely satirical portrait – Mrs Creevy cutting up the fried eggs at breakfast in order to serve them out with maximum advantage to herself, and handing Dorothy a list of 'good', 'medium' and 'bad' payers, so that her employee can calculate which girls it is safe to punish – which, inevitably, loses something in the relentlessness of its attack. The she-dragon, it is fair to say, has no life of her own.

Keep the Aspidistra Flying has its own minor version of Mrs Creevy. This is Mrs Wisbeach, the middle-aged gorgon who runs the boarding house at which Gordon lodges and whose life is spent in the constant enforcement of petty regulations – insisting that her 'gentlemen' be back to eat their meals at a certain time and don't smuggle women into their rooms. Elsewhere we are introduced to Gordon's sister Julia, a downtrodden drudge who works long hours in a genteel teashop and off whom he guiltily sponges, and Ravelston's girlfriend Hermione, praised for her beauty and style but with the intellectual capacity of a turnip. Rosemary, who may or may not have something to do with Eileen – although Orwell did not set eyes on his first wife until the novel was well under way – is a wonderful creation, charming, affectionate and long-suffering, even if the reader will probably wonder why such a bright, spirited girl would want to put up with irascible, egotistical, gloom-mongering Gordon; will wonder, too, about the marked air of male entitlement that hangs over Orwell's account of their relationship. From start to finish, it is Gordon's needs, Gordon's ambitions and Gordon's neuroses that count. You sometimes suspect that by the end of the book, Rosemary, newly married, living in an Edgware Road flat with a baby on the way and an unreliable husband, could have done better for herself.

Bowling in *Coming Up for Air* has none of Gordon's rebarbativeness. The reader sympathises with him, takes his side in the conflicts that characterise his life and groans with him in his dealings with the penny-pinching Hilda. Even so, there is no getting away from Bowling's contempt for his wife and the altogether sinister quality of his daydreams about her. 'I wonder whether you'll believe that during the first two or three years I had serious thoughts about killing Hilda,' he jauntily informs the reader after a brisk account of their courtship and marriage. On the other hand, as he reflects, one gets used to everything in time:

After a year or two I stopped wanting to kill her and started wondering about her. Just wondering. For hours, sometimes, on Sunday afternoons or in the evening when I've come home from work, I've lain on my bed with all my clothes on except my shoes, wondering about women. Why they're like that, how they get like that, whether they're doing it on purpose. It seems to be the most frightful thing, the suddenness with which some women go to pieces after they're married ... They don't want to have a good time, they merely want to slump into middle age as quickly as possible.

As for Hilda's peevish inertia, her husband knows exactly what has gone wrong. Like Flory with Elizabeth, Bowling has acquired enough information about his wife's early career to understand why she behaves in the way she does. As the daughter of a hard-up Anglo-Indian family trying to preserve their gentility in an inhospitable world, her life has been a constant struggle to make ends meet. Marriage is the only escape route available from the dreary, circumscribed world of her parents. Bowling knows this, but is still unable to forgive her for not conforming to the ideal he had of her when they met. It is the same with Elsie, his first love, whom he bumps into by chance behind the counter of a down-at-heel tobacconist's shop: 'It's frightening, the things that twenty-four years can do to a woman. Only twenty-four years, and the girl I'd known, with her milky-white skin and her red mouth and kind of dull-gold hair, had turned into this great round-shouldered hag, shambling along on twisted heels. It made me feel downright glad I'm a man. No man ever goes to pieces quite so completely as that.'

Not, of course, that Bowling is in the peak of physical condition. He is seriously overweight, wears false teeth and can't see his feet when he gets up out of the bath; as he concedes, no woman will ever look at him again unless she's paid to. Still, though, a faint scent of entitlement steals over these passages, the thought that women owe it to their menfolk to keep their physical attractiveness tuned up to the highest pitch. Girls may not be allowed to play, but they might at least keep themselves nice for the men who pay the bills and on whom the serious business of life naturally devolves.

◎

In filing these judgments, Orwell was merely expressing some of the commonplaces of his time. Most middle-class men at large in the interwar era did not expect rational thinking or common sense from the women they encountered, and one or two of Orwell's early letters show that he enjoyed playing up to this stereotype as a means of provoking his female correspondents. A letter to Brenda from 1934 notes that he has had lunch with an unidentified Dr Ede. 'He is a bit of a feminist and thinks that if a woman was brought up exactly like a man she would be able to throw a stone, construct a syllogism, keep a secret etc. He tells me that my anti-feminist views are probably due to Sadism!' On the other hand, the feminist case against Orwell tends to rest not on his novels – these, after all, are filled with fictional people whose views may not necessarily be those of their creator – but on the attitudes supposedly on display in *The Road to Wigan Pier*.

In his tour of the distressed industrial north, this argument runs, Orwell concerns himself largely with men who have been abandoned by the capitalist system. But there is a second, invisible army of the oppressed to whom his gaze barely turns. These are the women who sit at home worrying about how to feed their families and clothe their children – victims of a patriarchy whose keenest supporters are working-class men. It is undoubtedly true that most of the people Orwell writes about are men – miners, lodging-house keepers, trade union activists, the unemployed. At the same time, he is keenly alert to the consequences of female deprivation and oppression, as experienced by Mrs Searle, with whom he stays in Sheffield and where his efforts to help with the washing-up are disapproved of by the men, or the woman met at a dreadful caravan colony in Wigan, whose face bore 'a look of intolerable misery and degradation. I gathered that in that dreadful pigsty, struggling to keep her large brood of children clean, she felt as I should feel if I were coated all over with dung.'

And then there is *The Road to Wigan Pier*'s great symbolic moment – the slum girl Orwell sees from the window of the train bearing him away, on her knees in a wintry side alley trying to unblock a drain: 'She knew well enough what was happening to her – understood as well as I did how dreadful a destiny it was to be kneeling there in the bitter cold, on the slimy stones of a slum backyard, poking a stick up a foul drain-pipe.' The encounter has been slightly worked up – Orwell's diary confirms that he saw the girl in the street rather than from a railway carriage – but the effect is the same. The most significant memento that he brought back from the world beyond the Trent was a woman's face.

It is worth pointing out, too, that Orwell's views about most things not directly connected with politics tended to become more enlightened the longer he lived. Often this was a result of his having his deficiencies pointed out to him by friends. A long catalogue of remarks that might be construed as antisemitic came to an abrupt halt in the wake of a remonstrance from his Jewish friend Tosco Fyvel in 1945, after which Orwell seems to have gone out of his way to make amends for past incivility. It is the same with his attitude to women. Several of his 'As I Please' columns from the mid-1940s turn an interested and sympathetic eye on such topics as make-up or the contents of women's magazines, while a review of Woolf's *A Room of One's Own* notes that 'almost anyone of the male sex could read it to his advantage'. A dissection of some of the gender stereotyping on offer in *Vogue* in 1946 complains that 'Birth and death are not mentioned: nor is work, except that a few recipes for breakfast dishes are given. The male sex enters directly into perhaps one advertisement in twenty.' You suspect that at least some of Orwell's interest in society's expectations of women stemmed from his own involvement in what was traditionally regarded as a woman's role. Friends remarked on the enthusiasm he brought to the task of bringing up Richard after Eileen's death, but Orwell's childcaring abilities were in evidence from the moment of Richard's adoption. 'George is a good nurse-maid,' Lady Violet Powell once observed as he walked through her front door bearing a carrycot.

Sergeant Blair (top row, right) with members of the St John's Wood Home Guard.

8

ENGLAND

'BOYS' WEEKLIES' • 'CHARLES DICKENS' • 'INSIDE
THE WHALE' • *THE LION AND THE UNICORN* • *THE
ENGLISH PEOPLE* • *ANIMAL FARM* • *COMING
UP FOR AIR*

Orwell's writings on England and Englishness would fill a small volume in themselves. Indeed, *Orwell's England*, Peter Davison's Penguin selection from 2001, extends to over 400 pages. At various times, and in various contexts, he can be found examining English characteristics, English patriotism, English nationalism (and by extension English hypocrisy and English xenophobia), the English countryside, English cooking, English flora and fauna, English domestic interiors, English politics, English puritanism, English sports and pastimes (predominantly fishing), English murders, the English language, the English class system and English regional differences. *English*, you note: *The Lion and the Unicorn*, his famous war-era pamphlet, is subtitled *Socialism and the English Genius*; the rest of the British Isles could make their own arrangements. Although he spent much of the later 1940s living on Scottish soil, he despised, or affected to despise, the Scots: when sent a copy of Anthony Powell's verse satire *Caledonia* in 1936 he congratulated the author for 'calling them "Scotchmen", not "Scotsmen" as they like to be called. I find this a good easy way of annoying them.' Interestingly, this prejudice seems to have taken root during his time at St Cyprian's, part of whose snobbishness derived from its proprietors' fixation on such upper-class and quintessentially north-of-the-border pursuits as salmon-fishing and grouse-hunting.

In some ways this obsession with 'Englishness' – what it amounted to, the uses to which it might be put – is counterintuitive, or at least unexpected. The Blairs were originally Scottish. The Limouzins, his mother's family, came from France: with his toothbrush moustache and his dark hair, the adult Orwell has a markedly Gallic cast. It was his upbringing amid the South Oxfordshire verdure and at St Cyprian's and Eton, reading English classics and absorbing tales of military derring-do, that made him what he was. In one of the earliest photographs of him that survives, aged three, he is wearing a sailor suit, and one of his earliest memories was of being enrolled in the Navy League – a kind of pre-teen patriotic ginger group whose members were encouraged to shout the slogan 'We want eight [i.e. dreadnoughts] and we won't wait.' By his late thirties, he seems a quintessential English gentleman, dressed in shabby tweed, a devotee of traditional English cuisine, who brewed strong tea in an enormous pot that held a gallon of liquid and conversed in the curious top-down patois known as 'Duke of Windsor cockney', in which the words 'nothing whatever to do with it' came out as *nudding woddever to do wiv it.*

The same tendencies cover his attitude to books. He was keen on French literature (Villon, Baudelaire, Balzac, Zola) to the point of volunteering to translate it for publishers, and admired several contemporary Americans (Jack London, Henry Miller), but his real enthusiasm is mostly reserved for English writers: apart from an early 1930s love-affair with James Joyce, it is Chaucer, Shakespeare, Dickens, Thackeray, Gissing and Lawrence who are the stars of the show. Similarly, when it comes to England, his fondness for laying down the law and minting eye-catching generalisations about millions of people reaches its zenith: it is 'like a family with the wrong members in control', he remarks in *The Lion and the Unicorn*. Even when England is not his primary subject, it is always there by default, lurking in the margins or making its presence felt in unexpected ways. One sees this in *Burmese Days*, where England is invariably there as a yardstick by which the backdrops of South-east Asia can be judged and found wanting. Just as Flory's favourite season is the short winter when Upper Burma 'seemed haunted by the ghost of England' (the wildflowers are 'not quite the same as the English ones, but very like them'), so Orwell himself was irritated by the local landscapes. 'There is really nothing duller than a forest country in which every inch is covered by beastly creepers etc.,' he complained to Eleanor Jaques. 'I used to feel that very much in Burma . . . It used to oppress me that nothing seemed quite of the right kind – e.g. there was hardly any proper grass and a stream never had any proper banks but seeped off at the edges into beastly mangrove swamps etc.'

England, the implication runs, does these things better: the grass grows abundantly and the streams are properly defined. This is Orwell himself talking, but the same feelings are channelled into his novels. Throughout *Burmese Days* there rises an almost desperate air of yearning for 'home' that is as much Orwell's as Flory's. The latter has lived in Burma for a decade and a half without furlough. Now he is 'pining for England, though he dreaded facing it, as one dreads facing a pretty girl when one is collarless and unshaven'. His aim is to find a 'civilised girl' who is not repelled by his birthmark, marry her and eventually return to England, where they can 'buy a cottage in the country, surround themselves with friends, books, their children, animals'. Flory, as an unwilling servant of the Raj, is keen to throw off the shackles of imperialism: 'They would be free for ever of the smell of pukka sahibdom. He would forget Burma, the horrible country that had come near to ruining him.' Orwell's accounts of his own return to England after trips abroad are suffused with exactly the same scent. On the way back from France in *Down and Out in Paris and London* he notes that 'I was so pleased to be getting home, after being hard up for months in a foreign city, that England seemed to me a sort of Paradise.' There follows a list of the things Orwell really appreciates about his native land. It includes such staples of domestic comfort as bathrooms and armchairs, but most of the advantages are culinary: mint sauce, new potatoes properly cooked, brown bread, marmalade and 'beer made with veritable hops'.

At the end of *Homage to Catalonia* the tone turns yet more impassioned: 'And then England – southern England, probably the sleekest landscape in the world.' Travelling into London, with the rigours of Spain behind him and a bullet hole in his throat to remind him of all that he had gone through, Orwell notes that it was 'still the England that I had known in my childhood: the railway-cuttings smothered in wild flowers, the deep meadows where the great shining horses browse and meditate'. Simultaneously, there comes an acknowledgement that the vista he so eagerly descries is somehow embalmed, detached from reality, that everyone is really asleep, 'sleeping the deep, deep sleep of England, from which I sometimes fear that we will never wake until we are jerked out of it by bombs'. Strictly speaking, Orwell's enthusiasm for England and his interest in its institutions tends to increase as the decade progresses. *Coming Up for Air*, for example, is practically awash with elegiac descriptions of the Oxfordshire back lanes and the hidden pools with their giant carp. There are two reasons, you suspect, for this absorption in the minutiae of bygone English life. The first is that Orwell wrote most of the novel while staying in Morocco, whose landscape he disliked ('a beastly dull country, no forests and literally no wild animals', he told Cyril Connolly). The second is that, with war in prospect, he was nervous of its likely effect on the country he loved so much.

Here, in mid-1939, the idea of 'England' starts to move sharply into focus in Orwell's work. 'Boys' Weeklies' and 'Charles Dickens', two of the essays that, together with the title piece, would make up *Inside the Whale* (1940), are effectively studies in nationhood, with deep-seated implications for the kind of person Orwell had been and would become. The first, which may be said to have established Orwell's credentials as a literary sociologist – 'Please tell me who is George Orwell?' *Horizon*'s proprietor Peter Watson demanded of its editor, Connolly. 'His article is *splendid*' – is a study of some of the influences brought to bear on the formation of popular taste, in which Orwell seizes on newsagents' shops as a repository 'of what the mass of the English people really feels and thinks'. Naturally, there are guilty men: Orwell is convinced that the inherent conservatism of the magazines bought by teenage boys is directly connected to the political views of the press magnates who own them. Running beneath 'Boys' Weeklies', on the other hand, is a stealthy acknowledgement that many a grown-up, and possibly even Orwell himself, is implicated in the seductive vision of a bygone world offered up by *Magnet* and *Gem* and the misadventures of Billy Bunter, the Fat Owl of the Remove.

At one point, for example, Orwell attempts to sum up the mental atmosphere evoked by Charles Hamilton, Bunter's creator under the pen name Frank Richards:

The year is 1910 – or 1940, but it is all the same. You are at Greyfriars, a rosy-cheeked boy of fourteen in posh, tailor-made clothes, sitting down to tea in your study in the Remove passage after an exciting game of football which was won by an odd goal in the last half-minute. There is a cosy fire in the study and outside the wind is whistling. The ivy clusters thickly round the old grey stones. The King is on his throne and a pound is worth a pound. Over in Europe the comic foreigners are jabbering and gesticulating, but the grim grey battleships of the British fleet are steaming up the Channel and at the outposts of Empire the monocled Englishmen are holding the n——rs at bay.

That Orwell was emotionally invested in this world scarcely needs saying: Connolly's comment that he was 'a revolutionary in love with

1910' may well have been inspired by this very paragraph. Within the space of a couple of pages, the associative net is pulled even tighter. People are more influenced by popular entertainment than they would admit, Orwell suggests; the worst books are often the most important because they are usually the ones that are read earliest in life. It is probable that many of us are carrying through life 'an imaginative background which they acquired in childhood'. So, transparently, was Orwell himself.

'Charles Dickens', too, is an intensely personal document, in which Orwell can be seen busily quarrying material from the work of one of his favourite authors as a way of establishing his own position with regard to the British body politic. He begins by trying to rescue Dickens from the clutches of one or two of the critics who, in the past couple of decades, have tried to reinvent him: from G.K. Chesterton, who thought him 'almost a Catholic', and the Marxist writer T.A. Jackson, who identified him as a proto-revolutionary. What does Orwell find to admire in the author of *David Copperfield*? To begin with, he sees him as 'a subversive writer, a radical, one might truthfully say a rebel', but one whose complaints about the institutions he disliked tended to be greeted with enthusiasm even by the people he was attacking. And yet, as Orwell is quick to point out, his remedies for the problems of poverty, cruelty and discrimination are largely moral. If those in positions of power behaved differently, life would be better: it is as simple, or as complicated, as that.

From one angle, this is a point in Dickens's favour: 'the vagueness of his discontent is the mark of its permanence'. Victorian contemporaries such as Charles Reade, who wrote novels protesting about specific abuses, have already fallen off the map. Dickens's drawback is his inability to follow his deductions about national life through to their logical conclusions. The gloomy novels of his middle period may be all about the helplessness of individual characters in a corrupt society, but 'it was quite beyond him to grasp that, given the existing form of society, certain evils *cannot* be remedied'. To counter this is

Dickens's adherence to the 'English puritan tradition' in which he was born: narrow and sometimes emotionally stifling, perhaps, but devoid of 'vulgar nationalism' and 'typical English boasting'. He is an Englishman, but almost without being aware of the fact: 'He has no imperialist feeling, no discernible views on foreign politics, and is untouched by the military tradition.' Above all, he is able to give voice to what Orwell calls 'the native decency of the common man', the idea of 'freedom and equality' that has penetrated to 'all ranks of society'.

Dickens, then, is a nineteenth-century liberal, a free intelligence, whose attitude to life Orwell warmly commends while (you infer) wanting it to go further and to set about restructuring English life in a much more systematic way. Meanwhile, *Inside the Whale*'s title essay offers a third examination of 'Englishness', if only because its subject – by way of the American novelist Henry Miller – turns out to be the development of English literary politics in the period between 1910 and 1940. Orwell was a fan of Miller's *Tropic of Cancer* (1935); he had met Miller on his way to Spain at Christmas 1936, and had first-hand experience of the shiftless 'bohemian' end of the US expatriate community in 1920s Paris from which Miller drew his characters; Orwell introduces aspects of it into both *Down and Out in Paris and London* and *A Clergyman's Daughter*. Naturally, he admires Miller for writing a novel about *l'homme moyen sensuel* – George Bowling is a less debased version of this ideal – but also for his linguistic experiments, in which English is not only treated as a 'spoken' language, but spoken without fear, 'i.e. without fear of rhetoric or of the unusual or poetic word'.

Yet Miller is important to Orwell not only for his command of language, but also for the way in which his work taps into a tradition of 'freedom' which Orwell spends several of his later essays commending. 'Inside the Whale' has barely reached its half-dozenth page before Orwell launches into a terrific paean to Walt Whitman, from whom he imagines Miller to descend. To Whitman and the nineteenth-century American settlers that he wrote about, 'liberty' was not merely a highly desirable abstract, but something available at the end of every prairie track.

The democracy, equality and comradeship that Whitman is always talking about are not remote ideals Orwell suggests, but something that existed in front of his eyes. In mid-nineteenth-century America men felt themselves to be free and equal, so far as that is possible outside a society of pure communism. There was poverty and there were even class distinctions, but except for the Negroes (as the US black population was then commonly known), there was no permanently submerged class. Everyone had inside him a kind of core, the knowledge that he could earn a decent living, and earn it without bootlicking.

It scarcely needs saying that, as a summary of the early American experience, this is hopelessly romanticised – while altogether ignoring the Native Americans who had been displaced to make way for it – but Miller's Whitmanesque traits, an 'acceptance' of things that incorporates an acknowledgement that 'ordinary everyday life consists far more largely of horrors than writers of fiction usually care to admit', are, to Orwell, a vital part of his appeal. Even more important is that they offer an escape route from literary fashion and 'the general development of English literature in the twenty years since the Great War'. Miller's great merit is that he bears no resemblance to all the homegrown talents that Gordon Comstock spends the opening chapter of *Keep the Aspidistra Flying* so roundly excoriating.

There follows a brisk summary of the rise of 'commitment' in English letters, beginning with Orwell's boyhood hero A.E. Housman, whose verse, he is forced to concede, 'just tinkles', and moving on to the modernist titans of the 1920s – Joyce, Eliot, Pound and Lawrence. By and large, these writers are pessimists, but their sense of 'purpose' is 'very much up in the air'. They pay no attention to the urgent problems of the world, and the world-weariness that leaks out of their books is, paradoxically, the result of prosperity. 'Disillusionment was all the rage,' Orwell writes of the literary 1920s. 'Everyone with a safe £500 a year turned highbrow and began training himself in *tedium vitae*.' Why then the sudden rise of the Auden–Spender–MacNeice gang in the early 1930s, with their 'serious purpose', their left-wing message, their overwhelming air of uplift and – Orwell rams this point home – their willingness to subscribe to a form of Soviet-inflected socialism that 'makes mental honesty impossible'? For Orwell, the ranks of superannuated public schoolboys who made up so much of the literary left in the 1930s are a social as much as a political phenomenon: members of the newly unemployable middle classes, denied their berths in conventional professions by the austerity of the interwar era. To them the Communist Party is 'simply something to believe in', and their avowal of its doctrines 'the patriotism of the deracinated'.

Auden's famous line in his poem 'Spain' about accepting guilt in the necessary murder comes in for particular criticism: 'Mr Auden's brand of amoralism is only possible if you are the kind of person who is always somewhere else when the trigger is pulled.' Invoking the theory of permanent adolescence featured in Connolly's *Enemies of Promise*, with its elegies for bygone schooldays and lost adolescent love, he convicts most of the new movement of English writers of the crime of not having grown up. Miller, ultimately, is praised for his matter-of-factness: whether or not his work is an expression of what people ought to feel, 'it probably comes somewhere near to expressing what they *do* feel'. At the same time, you can sense Orwell's unease. Whatever the public uses to which it is put, in the end literature has a life of its own. 'On the whole,' he concludes, 'the literary history of the thirties seems to justify the opinion that the writer does well to keep out of politics.' Miller's quietism is justified. But Orwell is a political animal, who believes that all art is propaganda, that writers have a duty to engage with the landscapes around them and that, however arresting at the time, the modernist classics of the 1920s lacked something for being written in an atmosphere of economic security. Moreover, the essay was taking shape at a time when his own political opinions were undergoing a profound change. When the two men met in Paris in December 1936, Miller had told him in no uncertain terms that his journey to Spain to fight for the Republic was a futile gesture, and that as a writer he would have been better off staying at home and saving his skin. The author of *Tropic of Cancer* would doubtless have been equally unimpressed by Orwell's decision to support the Allied war against Nazi Germany. As it was, the first year of warfare provoked a radical restatement of Orwell's views on England and Englishness which framed them in a specifically political context. This was *The Lion and the Unicorn*, begun at the height of the Battle of Britain, completed during the Blitz, published in pamphlet form early in 1941 as part of Secker & Warburg's Searchlight Books series, and essentially a manifesto for left-wing political and social change.

The extent of Orwell's radicalism can be measured by several pieces he wrote about the newly formed Home Guard, formerly the Local Defence Volunteers, in the winter of 1940–1. To Orwell this body clearly has the potential to be a people's army. A *Tribune* piece of December 1940 notes that 'a million men with rifles in their hands are always important' and the opportunity such an organisation presents is 'so obvious that it is amazing that it has not been grasped earlier'. We are in a strange period of history, Orwell declares, 'in which a revolutionary has to be a patriot and a patriot has to be a revolutionary'. All this feeds into *The Lion and the Unicorn*, which not only seeks to isolate various English national characteristics but also discusses the political uses to which they can be put. Orwell begins by insisting that nations are individually distinct. Thus an Englishman who returns home from a foreign trip will immediately notice its singularity: 'The beer is bitterer, the coins are heavier, the grass is greener, the advertisements are more blatant.' But much of England's distinctiveness is negative. The English, he maintains, are not artistically gifted. Neither are they intellectually minded or interested in abstract ideas. Their essential nature may be located in two of their most deep-rooted characteristics: gentleness and a love of flowers.

This is a mostly private world, rooted in hobbies, quiet domesticity, distrust of interfering authority or prying eyes ('nosey-parkers'), where the genuinely popular culture rumbles on beneath the surface.

As ever, several of Orwell's generalisations about the English can be called seriously into question. At one point he asserts that ordinary people are 'without definite religious belief and have been so for centuries'. In fact, church attendances in the 1930s ran at 30 per cent of the population. Again, diagnosing a general dislike of war and militarism, he claims that 'they do not retain among their historical memories the name of a single military victory'. Agincourt? Trafalgar? Waterloo? The relief of Mafeking? And yet the final portrait, for all the deliberate picturesqueness of its snapshots – 'The clatter of clogs in the Lancashire mill towns, the to-and-fro of the lorries on the Great North Road, the queues outside the Labour Exchanges, the rattle of pin-tables in the Soho pubs, the old maids biking to Holy Communion through the mists of the autumn mornings' – is oddly resonant. England is, or was, like that, you feel. Orwell has somehow triumphantly taken the measure of it, established the basis of what makes it work, balanced the things he dislikes about it – hypocrisy about the profits of empire, the lack of genuine democracy – with its capacity for collective action, the 'emotional unity' it can suddenly discover when the chips are down, the 'subtle network of compromises' brought together to sustain it. England, he decides, in the famous metaphor that returns us to English privacy and English domesticity, is a family where power has been allowed to fall into the hands of the wrong people.

A family, more to the point, whose younger or more circumspect members need to take decisive action if it is to survive the buffetings of a new and more autocratic world. The lesson of the early twentieth century, as Orwell sees it, is that capitalism does not work. Fascism might be morally repugnant, but it succeeds 'because it is a planned system geared to a planned purpose . . . and not allowing any private interest, either of capitalist or worker, to stand in its way'. At which juncture *The Lion and the Unicorn* stops being a study of national temperament and transforms itself into a call for revolution:

> Almost certainly the mass of the people are now ready for the vast changes that are necessary; but those changes have not even begun to happen ... What is wanted is a conscious open revolt by ordinary people against inefficiency, class privilege and the rule of the old ... That means that there will have to arise something that has never existed in England, a Socialist movement that actually has the mass of the people behind it.

If, as Orwell maintains, only socialist nations can fight effectively, then the immediate priority is to turn the struggle against Nazi Germany 'into a revolutionary war and England into a Socialist democracy'. Curiously, 'The English Revolution', which offers suggestions as to how this may be achieved, is by far *The Lion and the Unicorn*'s weakest section. The tone turns hectoring, and the shrewdness of Orwell's dissections of nationhood gives way to straightforward stereotyping ('Once check that stream of dividends that flows from the bodies of Indian coolies to the banking accounts of old ladies in Cheltenham, and the whole sahib–native nexus, with its haughty ignorance on one side and envy and servility on the other, can come to an end,' etc., etc.). Naturally, there are several things to say in Orwell's defence. He was writing at a time of grave national peril when there seemed every chance that Britain might be overrun, amid a political and military situation whose later development could barely be guessed at. Orwell later came to acknowledge that he had overestimated the strength of revolutionary feeling in 1940 and that few of his predictions had been accurate. Significantly, his last major statement on 'Englishness', 15,000 words of letterpress for an illustrated volume entitled *The English People*, written in the autumn of 1943 but not published until nearly four years later, is a much more downbeat affair.

There are the usual remarks about artistic insensibility, the gentleness of the English crowds, the absence of a revolutionary tradition, the respect for the processes of law, but at the essay's core lies an almost rueful acceptance of the fact that the vast majority of English people are only interested in politics in so far as they affect their material needs. Bipartisan enthusiasm about the principles of the Beveridge Report of 1942, which set out the foundations of the post-war welfare state, is seen as evidence of a blurring of party distinctions. Just as the modern Tory party would never revert to what would have been called Conservatism in the nineteenth century, so no socialist government would ever massacre the monied classes or even confiscate their property without compensation. Class distinctions remain, but are liable to be confused by the rise of new and unplaceable managers and technocrats with less reverence for tradition and precedent who live in areas where the old social patterns have broken down. *The Lion and the Unicorn* ended with a clarion call to seize the day: 'we must grow greater or grow less'. Three years later, Orwell can only manage a cautious, medium-term prognosis: the next decade will make it clear whether England can survive as a great nation or not. If the answer is yes, 'it is the common people who will make it so'. Bets are being hedged; a vote of confidence will have to wait.

◎

By the time he sat down to write *The English People* in the early autumn of 1943, the first two phases of Orwell's wartime life were nearly over. Pronounced unfit for any kind of military service, he had spent the period 1939–41 working desultorily as a freelance journalist, before landing a job as a talks producer at the BBC's Eastern Service. Initial enthusiasm swiftly turned to rank disillusion – he once wrote that the tasks on which he was engaged were not useless but worse than useless – and in November 1943 he left the BBC to become literary editor of *Tribune*. This was a part-time position, allowing him time to write, and within a week of his arrival he was able to inform his agent that 'You will be glad to hear that I *am* writing a book again at last', adding that 'The thing I am doing is quite short, so if nothing intervenes it should be done in 3 or 4 months.' Orwell kept to his schedule and completed the manuscript by the early spring of 1944, but it would be another year and a half before the 100 or so pages of what became *Animal Farm* saw the light. Orwell's worry, expressed to his academic friend Gleb Struve, that 'it is so not OK politically that I don't feel certain in advance that anyone will publish it', was borne out by a series of rejections by major publishing houses, including Gollancz, who could not stomach its anti-Soviet satire at a time when Russia figured as an ally in the fight against Hitler. Even when Secker & Warburg, who had brought out both *Homage to Catalonia* and *The Lion and the Unicorn*, agreed to take it on, paper shortages delayed publication until August 1945.

Orwell described *Animal Farm* as 'a fairy story but also a political allegory'. As such, its succinct (and frequently humorous) account of a gang of animals who overthrow their human master and restructure his domain on egalitarian lines offers an alternative version of several decades of recent Russian history. Each major character has a real-life equivalent. Old Major, whose vision of a world in which animals can be free and equal, echoes the groundwork of Marx and Lenin. Napoleon (Stalin) and Snowball (Trotsky), who command the Bolshevik pigs until their inevitable falling-out, are supported by their proletarian allies (horses, cows, goats) in the defeat of Mr Jones, the farmer (Tsar Nicholas II). Thereafter, each of the novel's major episodes has a parallel in Soviet history in the period 1917–43. The Russian Civil War is echoed in Mr Jones's attempt to recapture the farm in the Battle of the Cowshed. There is a sinister burlesque of the Moscow Show Trials in which certain of the pigs are forced to confess to having been in league with the exiled Snowball. Law and order is the responsibility of a pack of savage dogs (the NKVD) bred up since puppyhood by the ever more autocratic Napoleon. Alliances with the rival farmers Mr Pilkington and Mr Frederick (Britain and America) are symbolised by the final scene in which the by now anthropomorphised pigs entertain their neighbours to dinner – a pastiche of the Tehran Conference of November 1943 in which the allied leaders Roosevelt, Stalin and Churchill convened to discuss the fate of the post-war world.

At the same time, as well as offering a satire of the Russian Revolution, *Animal Farm* has a second story going on beneath its surface. For this is an *English* rebellion, taking place in a recognisably English locale. A possible influence is Gissing's early novel *Demos: A Story of English Socialism* (1886), in which a working-class man inherits a fortune and tries to establish a rural commune run on egalitarian lines. Among various points of contact, the novel features a meeting at a socialist club where one of the speakers invites those present to visualise what such a community might look like in tones very similar to Old Major's exhortations ('Imagine such a happy land, my friends ...'). Even more significant, perhaps, is a scene towards the end when at an assembly to mark the scheme's unsuccessful closure a character complains that 'we're a poor lot and deserve to be worse treated than the animals that haven't the sense to use their strength'.

The importance of *Animal Farm*'s backdrop looms even larger when the reader comes to examine its chronology. When and where is it set? The Russian Revolution proceeded throughout the 1920s and 1930s, but the events of Orwell's novel belong to a much earlier period. The farm, for example, is completely unmechanised. There is scarcely any mention of motorised transport. As for the domestic interiors, the Joneses' drawing room is full of looking-glasses, horsehair sofas and Brussels carpets, and ornamented by a lithograph of Queen Victoria. The suspicion that all this is taking place in the very early years of the twentieth century is reinforced by incidental references to 'gentleman farmers', low-crowned bowler hats and governess carts – all of which suggest a grounding in the rural life of the

Edwardian era. The newspapers and magazines that the pigs take include the *Daily Mirror, Tit-Bits* and *John Bull* – a highly patriotic weekly that achieved its highest circulation during the Great War. Even the distinctively named solicitor Mr Whymper looks as if he was inspired by Orwell's memory of the celebrated Victorian mountaineer Edward Whymper, who died in 1911. As for Manor Farm's location, Willingdon, the nearby town, borrows the name of a village near Eastbourne, the home of St Cyprian's, but it sounds very like Henley-on-Thames, in whose vicinity Orwell spent much of his boyhood. As well as having the villains of the Soviet Revolution in his sights, Orwell also seems to be in hot pursuit of his childhood.

But *Animal Farm* has another subtext burrowing away beneath its surface. This is Orwell's attitude to the natural world and the species who populate it. The novel ends with the non-pig population of Manor Farm secretly monitoring the climax of a card game in which Napoleon and Mr Pilkington have simultaneously played the ace of spades. To their fascinated observers, man and pig are now interchangeable: 'Twelve voices were shouting in anger, and they were all alike. No question, now, what had happened to the faces of the pigs. The creatures outside looked from pig to man, and from man to pig, and from pig to man again; but already it was impossible to say which was which.'

Several animals emerge with no credit whatsoever from *Animal Farm*. Mollie the white mare, who wants to know if there will be sugar after the rebellion, shirks her duties, is seen fraternising with the enemy, disappears from her stall and is eventually discovered behind the shafts of a publican's dogcart. Benjamin the donkey is a case-hardened pessimist, as stolidly indifferent to conditions under the new regime as he was to the tyranny of Farmer Jones. Moses the raven tries to undermine the animals' loyalty with enticing tales of the paradisal never-never land of Sugar Candy Mountain. The sheep are credulous dimwits, whose only function is to chant their approval for Napoleon's self-aggrandising schemes, while the Manor Farm cat is swiftly revealed as an opportunist, keener on eating local birdlife and rabbits than on welcoming them into the communal fold. In the end, though, these turn out to be minor transgressions. With the exception of Snowball – a far-sighted visionary, whom Napoleon promptly chases off into exile – it is the pigs who are the villains of the piece.

Item one on an extensive charge sheet is the wholesale betrayal of revolutionary principle and the substitution of collective decision-making with a wool-pulling autocracy. Item two is the assassination, with maximum savagery, of political opponents. Item three is a consistent disregard for the concept of objective truth that expresses itself in regular rewrites of history whenever an inconvenient fact needs to be suppressed. But this is only the tip of an iceberg of callous porcine depravity. To tyranny, violence, duplicity and falsehood can be added hypocrisy, drunkenness, promiscuity ('In the autumn the four sows had all littered about simultaneously, producing thirty-one young pigs between them. The young pigs were piebald and as Napoleon was the only boar on the farm, it was possible to guess at their parentage'), deception and – we infer – cheating at cards. The pigs may be clever, resourceful and tactically astute, good at building windmills, playing off one neighbour against another, brewing beer and learning to walk on their hind legs, but all their expertise is put to malign ends. Orwell, clearly, loathes them from the start.

This detestation is all the more remarkable for the personal context from which it emerges. In terms of twentieth-century literary history, Orwell is the animal lover *par excellence*, as obsessed and enlivened by the traffic of hedgerow and pasture as many a paid-up 'nature' writer. Some of his best experiences had been with animals, he once remarked with an entirely straight face. His correspondence from the 1930s is crammed with excited reportage from nature rambles, ornithological despatches, expeditions in search of puss moths on Hayes Common; the baby hedgehogs who strayed into his parents' house in Southwold were assured of the warmest of welcomes. Significantly, this enthusiasm had a practical side. Fetched up in the Wallington cottage after the journey that produced *The Road to Wigan Pier*, he immediately set about establishing a smallholding, purchased a pair of goats and a crate of hens, subscribed to the *Farmer and Stockbreeder*, and seems to have regarded himself as a modern-day Tolstoy set down on the East Anglian flat.

And distance made the heart grow fonder. Convalescing in French Morocco in the winter of 1938–9, seriously unwell and alarmed by the disintegrating international situation, half his letters home are to Jack Common, the Hertfordshire neighbour housesitting for him in Wallington and tasked with looking after the livestock. Has Muriel the goat been mated with the neighbour's billy? Are the feed suppliers still delivering? All this is plainly quite as important to Orwell as the Munich crisis or the state of his lungs. And yet, for all the optimistic schemes for expanding the chicken population and renting additional land in the village, the Orwell smallholding always harbours a significant absence, a gaping hole which most small farmers of the time would have hastened to fill. Where is the pig? We know that Orwell was conscious of this deficiency. In *Coming Up for Air*, written during his stay in North Africa, George Bowling finds himself camped out at a munitions dump in Cornwall towards the end of the 1914–18 war in the company of a deaf old man named Private Lidgebird. A one-time market gardener, Lidgebird is rapidly reverting to type: 'Even before I got to Twelve Mile Dump he'd dug a patch round one of the huts and started planting spuds, in the autumn he'd dug another patch till he'd got about half an acre under cultivation, at the beginning of 1918 he'd started keeping hens … and towards the end of the year he suddenly produced a pig from God knows where.'

The pig, you infer, is the smallholder's calling card, his badge of authenticity, the item that grants his endeavours an air of seriousness. But where the fictional Private Lidgebird had led, the real-life Orwell did not yet care to follow. Clearly, he had observed pigs at close hand

– *Animal Farm* reveals a deep-rooted fascination with how farm life works, its routines, the hundred little details that keep the agricultural ship afloat. Equally clearly, he was not impressed by the behavioural quirks of pigs, and the distaste for pig life that flows into the novel played a substantial part in the difficulties he experienced in getting it published. Not only was the manuscript of *Animal Farm* turned down by several publishers in the spring and summer of 1944 on the grounds that a satire of our gallant Russian allies would be politically inopportune at a time when the Second World War was boiling up to crisis point, but turning Stalin and his henchmen into pigs compounded the offence. So did the fact that the pigs were obviously squandering their God-given talents. As T.S. Eliot put it in his letter from Faber & Faber rejecting the book, 'after all, your pigs are far more intelligent than the other animals, and therefore the best qualified to run the farm – in fact, there couldn't have been an Animal Farm at all without them'.

What was needed, Eliot gently chided him, was not more communism but more public-spirited pigs. Orwell's reaction to this piece of fatuousness is not recorded. But at the same time he was getting ready to bite the bullet, to take a decisive step that could not have been pursued either at Wallington or at the villa in Morocco, where despite his ill health he immediately began fashioning coops and living quarters for the chickens and goats that quickly followed him there. For on the Inner Hebridean island of Jura, where he rented a remote farmhouse between 1946 and 1948, a pig finally made an appearance among the ranks of livestock. What does Orwell think of this animal? One mark of his distaste is the fact that the pig seems never to have been named. Muriel the Wallington goat had made it into *Animal Farm*, but the Jura pig is simply 'the pig' – although this anonymity may simply have stemmed from an acknowledgement of its fate; Muriel, after all, was not being bred up for slaughter. Part of Orwell is impressed by its ability to thrive in what were less than promising conditions: 'He has grown to a stupendous size on milk and potatoes, without our buying any food from outside,' he reported at one stage. But his fundamental dislike of the breed remained. 'For the first time in my life I have tried the experiment of keeping a pig,' he explained to a friend. 'They really are disgusting brutes and we are all longing for the day when he goes to the butcher.' With the exception of some criticisms of one of his mother's over-nourished dogs, this is the only occasion on which Orwell is known to have complained about an animal.

At the heart of this distaste was straightforward fastidiousness, a sensibility that for some reason could not tolerate the sight of the average pig in action. But when did Orwell decide that a pig could be anthropomorphised in the style of *Animal Farm*, or vice versa? *Coming Up for Air* contains a curious passage in which Bowling revisits Lower Binfield, the Oxfordshire town in which he was brought up:

> At the other end of the market-place the High Street rises a little. And down this little hill a herd of pigs was galloping, a huge flood of pig-faces. The next moment, of course, I saw what it was. It wasn't pigs at all, it was only the schoolchildren in their gas-masks. I suppose they were bolting for some cellar where they'd been told to take cover in case of air-raids. At the back of them I could even make out a taller pig who was probably Miss Todgers. But I tell you that for a moment they looked exactly like a herd of pigs.

Orwell maintained that he got the idea for *Animal Farm* sometime in 1937 when he saw a small boy directing a carthorse down a country lane and wondered what would happen if the horse refused to play ball. But you suspect that the real prod came sometime the following year. Orwell spent the spring and summer of 1938 at a sanatorium near Aylesford in Kent recovering from a life-threatening haemorrhage. Mounting panic about war and the probability of gas attacks – a government adviser had predicted a quarter of a million deaths in the first week of hostilities – had already prompted the widespread distribution of gas masks. It seems a reasonable assumption that at some point during his stay, perhaps on one of his visits to Aylesford, he saw a crowd of gas mask-wearing children out in the street and made the connection that lies at *Animal Farm*'s pig-hating heart.

'I for one would be sorry to see them vanish' ('The Art of Donald McGill').

9

POPULAR CULTURE

COMING UP FOR AIR • 'THE ART OF DONALD MCGILL'
• 'DECLINE OF THE ENGLISH MURDER' • 'RAFFLES
AND MISS BLANDISH' • 'CRICKET COUNTRY' • 'THE
SPORTING SPIRIT' • 'THE MOON UNDER WATER'

Orwell always kept a sharp eye on the vagaries of popular culture. From the songs played on gramophones in the heat-sodden European clubs of 1920s-era Upper Burma (*Burmese Days*) to the specialist magazines on display in the public libraries of inner London (*A Clergyman's Daughter*) and the kind of slogans that screamed from mid-1930s advertising hoardings (*Keep the Aspidistra Flying*), his early work is full of fascinated glimpses into the unofficial and mostly unreported cultural lives of ordinary people. You sense that these accumulations of data appeal to him because 'official' culture, of the kind promulgated by the BBC and the highbrow weeklies, scarcely knows that they are there. Where else but in Orwell would you find mention of a publication called *Cage Birds* and its mysterious headlines ('Do bullies [i.e. bullfinches] thrive on rape [i.e. rapeseed]')? But the seeds of his longstanding professional interest in everyday recreations and mundane amenities were sown in *Coming Up for Air*, specifically in the chapters which describe George Bowling's early life in Lower Binfield around the time that the Victorian era was coming to a close.

Certainly the cultural detail of Bowling's childhood is laid on with a trowel, to the point that his adventures between the ages of six and sixteen often look as if they are about to drown beneath a tide of detail. There is something altogether irresistible about this absorption, as if Orwell can't stop himself, knows that his account of the confectionery available in the average Edwardian sweetshop is threatening to turn into a riot of superfluous information ('Sugar mice and sugar pigs were eight a penny, and so were liquorice pistols, popcorn was a halfpenny for a large bag, and a prize packet which contained several different kinds of sweets, a gold ring and sometimes a whistle, was a penny'), but is determined to press on regardless. It is the same with the clothes people wear, and particularly the glad rags in which fashion-conscious teenagers desperate to proclaim their maturity yearn to array themselves in the face of parental disapproval. Significantly, the moment at which Bowling's father tells him that he will have to leave school and get a job as a grocer's assistant swiftly develops into an argument about a new suit, with a kind of coat called a 'cutaway' that was fashionable in around 1910.

Nowhere is this fixation on Edwardian-era leisure pursuits more conspicuous than in Bowling's rhapsodising about fishing, a pastime by which he claims to have been totally absorbed from the ages of eight to fifteen. As with the sweetshop counter, there are long paragraphs about the paraphernalia of fishing – how to manufacture a hook, what to use for bait ('Boiled wheat isn't bad for roach. Redworms are good for gudgeon'), the two-shilling rod bestowed on him as a Christmas present in 1903. Fishing, to Bowling, is – literally – a backwater of serenity and silence, a place where modernity can be kept at bay and freedom of a sort lies endlessly to hand. Fishing, too, offers *Coming Up for Air* its great symbolic property, in the shape of the pool of giant carp, lost in the overgrown thickets of the Binfield Hall estate, which the adult Bowling pines to revisit, only to find it turned into a rubbish dump. Significantly, the act of casting a fishing rod into an Oxfordshire stream is also there to make a moral point.

There's a kind of peacefulness even in the names of English coarse fish. Roach, rudd, dace, bleak, barbel, bream, gudgeon, pike, chub, carp, tench. They're solid kind of names. The people who made them up hadn't heard of machine-guns, they didn't live in terror of the sack or spend their time eating aspirins, going to the pictures and wondering how to keep out of the concentration camp.

The same note rises from the famous essay on comic postcards, 'The Art of Donald McGill'. McGill's drawings, with their poster-paint colours, their enormous fat-bottomed women and their diminutive henpecked husbands, and their bedrock-level humour about mothers-in-law, courting couples and adultery, are fascinating in themselves, but they are also exercises in subversion, something that exists beyond the margins of formal English life, another barricade against those smelly little orthodoxies bent on suborning the individual consciousness to a regimented pattern.

◎

Coming Up for Air takes a lively interest in what, to Orwell, is another key aspect of popular culture: crime. Bowling's mother, it turns out, is an avid reader of Sunday newspapers and, as such, a terrified connoisseur of murder: 'I think Mother thought of the world outside Lower Binfield chiefly as a place where murders were committed. Murders had a terrible fascination for her, because, as she often said, she just didn't know how people could *be* so wicked.' Jack the Ripper, Mrs Manning, Dr Palmer, Crippen, who cut up his wife into pieces and buried her in the coal cellar – each of these celebrated Victorian murderers features in Mrs Bowling's private demonology ('How anyone could *do* such things!'). The shutters that adorn the family shopfront are a direct response to the Ripper scare, and born of a conviction that the murderer was hiding in Lower Binfield: 'Shutters for shop windows were going out, most of the shops in the High Street didn't have them, but Mother felt safer behind them.'

Jack the Ripper, Palmer and Crippen, together with Neill Cream, Mrs Maybrick, Seddon, Joseph Smith, Armstrong and Bywaters and Thompson, feature in 'Decline of the English Murder' (1946), in which Orwell considers what he calls the 'Elizabethan period' (this is put between 1850 and 1925), examines those murders 'whose reputation has stood the test of time' and then notes that 'the prevalent type of crime seems to be changing'. Most of the great cases he considers are revealed as essentially middle-class crimes, inspired by a desire for respectability, social position or the money necessary to acquire it. The archetypal murderer, as Orwell sees it, is likely to be a little man of the professional class, living an intensely respectable life, wracked by a guilty passion but with enough of a conscience to suffer mental agonies before the deed – planned with meticulous care, naturally – is done. All this, Orwell maintains, gives such crimes a dramatic, even a tragic quality, which as well as making them memorable awakens pity for both victim and murderer.

All this is in sharp contrast with the 'cleft chin murder', a wartime *cause célèbre*, in which an American army deserter and an eighteen-year-old former waitress deliberately ran over a young female cyclist, threw another girl into a river and, after murdering a taxi driver, spent the £8 they found in his pocket at the greyhound track. This, to Orwell, is a 'meaningless' story, due partly to the 'brutalizing effects of war' and, he suspects, a by-product of the Americanisation of British life. The great Victorian murderers might have committed heinous crimes, but they were the product of a stable society 'where the all-prevailing hypocrisy did at least ensure that crimes as serious as murder should have strong emotions behind them'. Interestingly, the argument about the moral consequences of American cultural influences is foreshadowed in 'Raffles and Miss Blandish' (1944). This compares the adventures of E.W. Hornung's 'amateur cracksman', a gentlemanly English burglar, with James Hadley Chase's *No Orchids for Miss Blandish* (1939), in which the daughter of an American millionaire is kidnapped and held to ransom by a band of brutish gangsters, gets to like the attentions of her chief abuser and, after her father's rescue posse has exterminated the kidnappers, flings herself out of a skyscraper window. Although he concedes that while obviously deriving from William Faulkner's *Sanctuary* (1931), *No Orchids* is well written, with not a word out of place, Orwell regards it as an exercise in pure fascism, in which ends will always conquer means and might always triumph over right. The devitalising effect of imported Americana continued to haunt him: he was particularly annoyed by shiny US magazines whose remit, as he saw it, was to proselytise on behalf of consumer materialism and pretend that no one ever dies.

◎

Popular culture was important to Orwell for the moral and political lessons that could be gleaned from it. Several of these could be seen to reside in sport. What did Orwell himself think about games-playing? A letter home from St Cyprian's records a stint as goalkeeper in a football match in which his opponents 'came at me like angry dogs', and he was remembered as a skilful centre-forward in competitions involving Burmese police teams. He was a notable performer in the Eton wall game. Boxing seems to have disgusted him: he was especially put out by the effect that watching a bout had on women. Tennis, played exclusively by expats, features in *Burmese Days* as a symbol of European superiority and in *Coming Up for Air* as a badge of class solidarity, played by the middle-class citizens of Ealing, where Bowling lives as a young man, to distinguish themselves from hoi polloi. Orwell's youthful love of cricket was reflected in an adult fixation on the annual Eton–Harrow match, which turns up several times in his diaries and letters; he was suitably awestruck at being allowed into the committee room at Lord's for a Home Guard meeting in the early years of the war.

In the whole of the Orwell canon, there are only two extended pieces about sport: a review of Edmund Blunden's *Cricket Country*, written for the *Manchester Evening News* in 1944, and 'The Sporting Spirit', which commemorates the Moscow Dynamo football team's tour of the UK in the autumn of 1945. As with fishing, Orwell's attitude to the cricket matches described in Blunden's elegy to a fading world is curiously double-edged, and his obvious love for the aesthetic pleasure of the old-style village game ('where everyone plays in braces, where the blacksmith is liable to be called away in mid-innings on an urgent job, and sometimes, about the time when the light begins to fail, a ball driven for four kills a rabbit on the boundary') runs side by side with an appreciation of what, in the modern age and in socio-political terms, cricket might be thought to stand for. Cricket, Orwell argues, is not an inherently snobbish game, as the twenty-five people needed to make up a fixture 'necessarily leads to a good deal of social mixing'. The truly snobbish pastime is golf, 'which causes whole stretches of countryside to be turned into carefully guarded class preserves'. Orwell's only complaint is cricket's tendency towards regimentation and ritualisation and the way in which thousands of reluctant schoolchildren are dragooned into playing it. The game was 'most truly rooted in the national life when it was voluntary and informal'.

'The Sporting Spirit', on the other hand, is concerned to build a bridge between sport and nationalism. Unimpressed by press reports of the four Moscow Dynamo matches ('encouraging young men to kick each other on the shins amid the roars of infuriated spectators'), Orwell is quick to locate these 'orgies of hatred' in the conviction that they are a form of 'mimic warfare'. Serious sport has nothing to do with fair play: 'It is bound up with hatred, jealousy, boastfulness, disregard of all rules and sadistic pleasure in witnessing violence: in other words it is war minus the shooting.'

As to how the modern cult of sport arose, 'there cannot be much doubt that the whole thing is bound up with the rise of nationalism – that is, with the lunatic modern habit of identifying oneself with large power units and seeing everything in terms of competitive prestige'. One doesn't have to be a paid-up football fan, much less an apologist for some of the modern game's excesses, to suspect that Orwell is overstating his case, and that he is ignoring football's emergence as the major leisure pursuit of the English working classes in the late nineteenth and early twentieth centuries; ignoring football generally, if it comes to that. Several critics of *The Road to Wigan Pier* have suggested that if Orwell had really wanted to immerse himself in the popular culture of the interwar-era industrial north he should have spent a Saturday afternoon on a soccer terrace. J.B. Priestley in his description of a football match in *The Good Companions* (1930) seems to comprehend the passions that a game can command after a week spent on the factory floor, and its importance to the local community; to Orwell, on the other hand, it is simply conflict without the hand grenades.

There are other areas of 'ordinary' life in which Orwell tries to show solidarity with his fellow citizens and somehow fails to connect. Take, for example, his fascination with pubs – the subject of two full-length pieces and countless incidental references. Gordon Comstock is (when in funds) an enthusiastic tippler whose night in the cells follows hard on the heels of a session spent downing beer by the quart. Bowling, too, is a saloon-bar habitué who spends much of his visit to Lower Binfield soaking in the hotel bar: 'The fact was that, what with a bottle of wine at lunch and another at dinner and several pints in between, besides a brandy or two, I'd had a bit too much to drink the day before.' And one of the most memorable scenes in *Nineteen Eighty-Four* finds Winston in a prole pub cross-questioning an old man about the world of half a century before (there are no pints in Oceania – the beer comes in litres and half-litres). Pubs are also there in Orwell's fiction to showcase skirmishes in the class war, with upper-class characters uncomfortably at large in an unfamiliar milieu soon exposing themselves as moonlighting toffs.

How did Orwell envisage the average pub? To judge from a review of a Mass Observation survey entitled *The Pub and the People*, published in 1943, he seems to have regarded it as a focus for collective entertainment. The survey's chief finding – that 'the pub as a cultural institution is at present declining' – is a source of intense regret: another example of the modern retreat from 'creative communal amusements' towards the 'passive, drug-like pleasures' of the cinema and the radio. 'The Moon Under Water', written three years later, takes this idea further by offering a paean to the ideal pub. Although it bears certain resemblances to a pub not far from his Islington flat, the establishment of the title is represented as a product of Orwell's imagination. As well as being hopelessly old-fashioned in design ('its whole architecture and fittings are uncompromisingly Victorian ... everything has the solid comfortable ugliness of the nineteenth century'), its usages are firmly located in a bygone age. Games are only allowed in the public bar; there is no radio and no piano; the barmaids – middle-aged women who call everyone 'dear' – know most of their customers by name and take a personal interest in their welfare.

Like the essay 'A Nice Cup of Tea', written for the same London *Evening Standard* series, the general tone is narrowly prescriptive. The Moon Under Water never makes the mistake of 'serving a pint of beer in a handleless glass', and is commended for having among its supply of glass and pewter mugs 'some of those pleasant strawberry-pink china ones which are seldom seen in London'. There is also a garden, which admits children and extends to family parties, and a dining room upstairs which offers 'a good, solid lunch – for example, a cut off the joint, two vegetables and boiled jam roll – for about three shillings'. Plainly, no pub in England could ever rise to all the exacting challenges Orwell has set down – towards the end of the article he notes rather sternly that 'I have mentioned above ten qualities that the perfect pub should have, and I know one pub that has eight of them' – but this is not the point. What remains is a quaint little vision of an almost archaic public amenity, awash with neighbourliness, solidity and communal good cheer.

Clearly Orwell regarded the pub as a flaring symbol of the virtues of down-market national life. How did he get on in them himself? Much of the evidence suggests that, though he was keen on spending time on licensed premises, Orwell was not really at home in them. His brother-in-law Humphry Dakin remembered escorting him to a pub in Leeds, where he sat on his own 'looking like death'. George Woodcock recalled him drinking at what may have been the model for the Moon Under Water, never managing to talk to anyone or seeming to fit in. Significantly, his strict adherence to the rituals of pub life seems to have been a part of his efforts to identify with the working classes: taking a colleague from the BBC named John Morris to a pub near Broadcasting House, he professed himself shocked to hear his companion ask for 'a glass of beer'. Morris had betrayed himself, Orwell quickly pronounced. A working-class customer would have asked for 'a glass of bitter'. Morris, who neither liked pubs nor considered himself working class, was mystified, unsure what point Orwell was trying to prove. But the point is the principle established in the review of *The Pub and the People*. Here was another 'creative communal amusement' of which Orwell, for all his solitariness and self-absorption, desperately wanted to become a part.

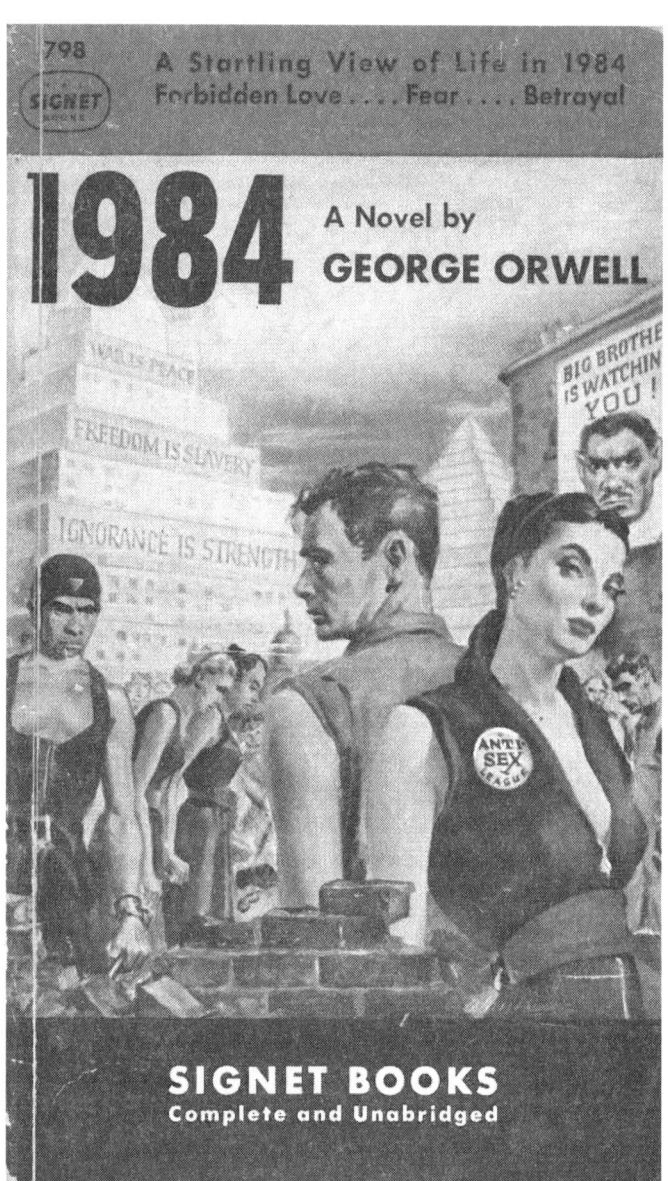

Big Brother as Stalin: the original Signet Books paperback of Nineteen Eighty-Four.

10

BIG BROTHER

'FREEDOM AND HAPPINESS' • 'YOU AND THE
ATOM BOMB' • 'SECOND THOUGHTS ON JAMES
BURNHAM' • 'THE PREVENTION OF LITERATURE' •
NINETEEN EIGHTY-FOUR

Animal Farm did not make Orwell famous, but it established his reputation as a writer in a way that none of his previous books had
been able to achieve. Its success, both in the UK and America, where
it was a Book of the Month Club selection, brought him financial
security: his earnings from the novel over the next four years would
amount to nearly £12,000. And yet in some ways its commercial and
critical triumph was an obstacle flung across his path rather than an
indication of the shape his future career might take. Orwell had always been a quick worker. None of his early novels took him much
more than a year. *A Clergyman's Daughter* had been written in nine
months. *Homage to Catalonia*, begun the moment he returned from
Spain in July 1937, was ready for the printer in February 1938. Come
the mid-1940s, on the other hand, the machine starts to slow down.
Nineteen Eighty-Four, which Orwell reckoned to have been inspired
by the Tehran Conference of November 1943, took five and a half
years to complete and publish in a creative process littered by false
starts and revisions: a few pages done in the summer of 1945; a more
sustained attempt in the summer of 1946; another recommencement

in the spring of 1947; more drafting and redrafting the following year. It was not until the end of 1948 that a final manuscript was complete.

There are several reasons for this catalogue of delay. The most obvious is the chaos surrounding Orwell's personal life. Eileen died unexpectedly on the operating table in March 1945 while her husband was away in occupied Europe working as a war correspondent for the *Observer* and the *Manchester Evening News*. The previous year, having despaired of their ability to conceive a child themselves, the couple adopted a newly born baby whom they named Richard Horatio Blair. Although he maintained an enviable – or dismaying – stoicism (Eileen 'wasn't a bad old stick', he told one friend), Orwell was deeply affected by her death. Determined to bring Richard up himself, he hired a nanny-cum-housekeeper named Susan Watson, installed her in his Islington flat and tried to renew a version of the domestic life he had previously enjoyed with his dead wife. One mark of his psychological distress during the winter of 1945–6 was his habit of proposing marriage, more or less on the spot, to any remotely eligible young woman who caught his eye. Without exception, the girls turned him down, although one of them, Sonia Brownell, at this point Connolly's understrapper on *Horizon*, would eventually change her mind shortly before his death.

To emotional meltdown could be added the question of Orwell's failing health. A long letter from April 1946 to Anne Popham, one of the women to whom he had fruitlessly proposed a couple of months before, suggests that 'What I am really asking you is if you would like to be the widow of a literary man. If things remain more or less as they are there is a certain amount of fun in this, as you would probably get royalties coming in and you might find it interesting to edit unpublished stuff etc.' Orwell goes on to maintain that 'there is no knowing how long I shall live', but he seems to have realised that his days were numbered. A few weeks before he had suffered a serious haemorrhage – Susan Watson had discovered him in the corridor of the Islington flat with blood pouring from his mouth –

and only managed to escape removal to a TB hospital by hood-winking the doctor who attended him and pretending that he had gone down with gastritis. The last four years of his life would be dominated by illness, fading strength and the need for long periods of rest and recuperation: the diary entries from the autumn of 1948 when he was struggling to finish *Nineteen Eighty-Four*'s final draft ('pain in side very bad') make grim reading. To complete a full-length novel would be a race against time.

Meanwhile, although *Nineteen Eighty-Four*'s outlines were clear in his head, he had no real idea of what ultimate shape the book might take. Any attempt to reconstruct the creative process that brought the novel from conception to execution involves a pile of evidence that goes back to the late 1930s. Spain, naturally, had offered Orwell a crash course in how a totalitarian state wields its power. Among a stack of inspirational books lay a chain of futurist novels that began with Wells, Huxley, London and Bramah and ended with his discovery of Yevgeny Zamyatin's *We* (1924), a legendary dysto-pian fantasy set in the twenty-sixth century which produced a *Tribune* essay entitled 'Freedom and Happiness' in January 1946. An exercise book containing notes for two projected novels entitled 'The Quick and the Dead' and 'The Last Man in Europe', compiled towards the end of the war, refers to 'Newspeak', the Party slogans ('War is Peace, Ignorance is Strength', 'Freedom is Slavery') and 'The Two Minutes Hate', all of which were to resurface five years later. Clearly *Nineteen Eighty-Four*'s key themes had been setting his imagination aflame for some time before he wrote its first few pages in the summer of 1945.

Where did Orwell stand politically in the last half-decade of his life? Although he kept a sceptical eye on the legislative programme of the newly elected Labour government, whose leader Clement Attlee he once described as resembling a dead fish that has just begun to stiffen, there is a suspicion that his real enthusiasm was now reserved for specific cases and causes. He was, for example, a great supporter of the Freedom Defence Committee and a regular attendee at its protest meetings. His anti-Sovietism remained a constant and explains his involvement in the activities of the Information Research Department (IRD), a branch of the Foreign Office which commissioned pamphlet literature for distribution in parts of Eastern Europe now falling under communist sway. Orwell's 'list' of public figures whom he suspected of pro-Russian sympathies, compiled for the IRD's Celia Kirwan, is sometimes held up as an example of Orwell's intolerance and a desire to censor the views of people with whom he disagreed. This is an exaggeration. As the IRD's brief was to produce pro-democracy pamphlets, it was vitally important that the writers involved should themselves be democrats. And while the list betrays a fair amount of personal animosity, many of the names on it belonged to politicians or journalists later revealed to be communist fellow travellers. 'Not very sensational', Orwell remarked to Celia when he sent it in: posterity would probably agree with him.

Significantly, much of Orwell's journalism from the period 1945–7 rehearses arguments or introduces material that would later make its way into the world of Airstrip One. 'You and the Atom Bomb', for example, published in *Tribune* in October 1945, canvasses the idea of 'zones of influence', a process by which the world was being 'parcelled off into three great empires, each self-contained and cut off from contact with the outer world, and each ruled, under one disguise or other, by a self-elected oligarchy'. Already the shades of Oceania, Eurasia and Eastasia are looming up through the mist. A second essay, about the American management guru James Burnham, which appeared the following spring, develops an argument brought parenthetically into *The Lion and the Unicorn* five years before: that the future will be controlled not so much by the dictator or the military strategist as by the technocrat. What is now creeping into view, Orwell decides after an examination of Burnham's *The Managerial Revolution* (1941), is a highly centralised and above all oligarchical world 'which will be neither capitalist nor, in any accepted sense of the word, democratic. The rulers of this new society will be the people who effectively control the means of production: that is, business executives, technicians, bureaucrats and soldiers.'

All this has an echo in the world of *Nineteen Eighty-Four*, which may be bossed by the Thought Police and buttressed by its military might, but is really controlled by people like O'Brien – circumspect bureaucrats ceaselessly striving to improve the logistics of a planned economy whose complexities are far too great for the ordinary citizen to grasp. Several other pieces from the immediate post-war period focus on what might be called the psychology of totalitarianism and the level of deception necessary for it to function. An introduction to a volume of short stories by Jack London notes 'that peculiar horror of totalitarian society, the way in which suspected enemies of the regime *simply disappear*'. Three years later Winston Smith will sit in the canteen at the Ministry of Truth reflecting on the likely future fate of his colleague Syme: 'One of these days, thought Winston with sudden deep conviction, Syme will be vaporised. He is too intelligent. He sees too clearly and speaks too plainly. The Party does not like such people. One day he will disappear. It is written in his face.' And Syme does indeed vanish: there comes a day when he is no longer at his desk, and it is as if he never was. Similarly, 'The Prevention of Literature', published in January 1946, discusses the 'organised lying' characteristic of totalitarian states. This, Orwell argues, is not incidental to the way in which autocracies wield their power, but a fundamental part of their strategy. Such is the level of deceit required by a despot to cover up his tracks and conceal his errors that administrative life involves a constant rewriting of history: 'Totalitarianism demands, in fact, the continuous alteration of the past, and in the long run probably demands a disbelief in the very existence of objective truth.'

Neatly enough, Winston Smith's professional life is founded on this very task. As a minor cog in the wheel of the Ministry of Truth's campaign to suppress the objective chronicling of the past, his job is to rewrite back numbers of *The Times*, endlessly recalibrating this official record of Oceanian life to accommodate forecasts that have proved inaccurate or to exclude notable personalities who have disgraced themselves. A specimen few minutes' work in his lonely cubicle involves reworking a since-disproved military prophecy, rectifying some output figures, and substituting for a 'categorical pledge' not to reduce the chocolate ration a warning that such a reduction was on the cards from the outset. While the world beyond the window consists of a never-ending military struggle in which the three great superpowers, Oceania, Eurasia and Eastasia, are permanently at war with each other, Winston's day-to-day life is a combination of boredom and fear, lived out in a highly corrosive atmosphere whose principal agents are language, surveillance technology and the unrelenting gaze of Oceania's leader, Big Brother, whose face stares from every poster. The advantage of Newspeak, Oceania's ever-more compressed official language, is – as Winston's dictionary-compiling colleague, the soon-to-be-vaporised Syme, enthuses – that 'in the end we shall make thoughtcrime literally impossible, because there will be no words in which to express it'.

But Winston is already embarked on his own particular thoughtcrime. His catalogue of misdemeanours begins when he buys an ancient notebook, full of 'smooth, creamy paper, a little yellowed by age, of a kind that had not been manufactured for at least forty years past', and, in defiance of Oceanian law – detection will mean punishment by 'death, or at least by twenty-five years in a forced-labour camp' – starts to keep a diary in which he scribbles the insurrectionary slogan 'DOWN WITH BIG BROTHER'. Emboldened by this small act of subversion, he begins an affair with a much younger woman named Julia, ornament of the Junior Anti-Sex League, and rents a love nest over an antique shop in which he and his girlfriend can examine a copy of Oceania's fabled banned book – *The Principles of Oligarchical Collectivism*, written by the exiled Trotsky figure Emmanuel Goldstein – presented to them by O'Brien, an apparently sympathetic member of the Inner Party and a stalwart of the 'Brotherhood', an underground organisation working for regime change.

Like every other novel Orwell wrote, *Nineteen Eighty-Four* is about a revolution that fails, about the rebel who is eventually returned to base and compelled to acknowledge the error of their ways. Flory in *Burmese Days* ends up killing himself. Dorothy in *A Clergyman's Daughter* finds herself back in her father's rectory engaged upon exactly the same futile tasks that were occupying her time when she left. Gordon in *Keep the Aspidistra Flying* marries Rosemary and, albeit half-unwillingly, resumes his worship of the money-god. George Bowling in *Coming Up for Air* knuckles down to life with the joyless Hilda. The non-porcine population of *Animal Farm* suffers the same indignities as it did in the days of Mr Jones. And so there is a terrible inevitability about the arrival of the Thought Police and Winston's removal to the Ministry of Love, where he is tortured with electric shocks, threatened with a cageful of starving rats that are about to be strapped over his face, and instructed by O'Brien – his chief tormenter – that his ordeal will only end once he can be got to genuinely believe that 2+2=5, rather than feigning to do so. The scenes in which O'Brien explains his reasoning to Winston amplify Bowling's conversation with Porteous in *Coming Up for Air*. The tyrants of old merely wanted to slaughter their enemies, but the modern autocrat has a much more insidious aim in view. He wants to change the way his opponents think.

O'Brien's role in *Nineteen Eighty-Four* is far from straightforward. He is there to tyrannise and bewilder, but also to coax and exhort and occasionally even to reassure. Winston is terrified of him, but also anxious to please him. His connection to the claustrophobic world of Sambo, Flip and St Cyprian's was first noted by Anthony West nearly seventy years ago. And yet there is a suspicion that the scenes at the Ministry of Love were inspired by an episode in Orwell's early career as a journalist. One might note, for example, that moment in which

O'Brien, having administered the first of several electric shocks to his victim, becomes 'less severe' and is said to have the air of 'a doctor, a teacher, even a priest'. He is taking trouble with Winston, he informs his hapless victim, because he is 'worth trouble'.

All this has a curious echo of an incident in which a Catholic priest can be found taking trouble with Orwell the apprentice book reviewer. In June 1932, six months before the publication of *Down and Out in Paris and London*, Orwell filed a notice of Karl Adam's *The Spirit of Catholicism* for the *New English Weekly*. The piece also refers to C.C. Martindale's *The Faith of the Roman Church* (1927), which Orwell mistranscribes as *The Roman Faith*. Adam's book is favourably compared with Martindale on the grounds that 'the contrast between the Catholic who simply believes and the convert who must forever be justifying his conversion, is like the contrast between a Buddha and a performing fakir'. Father Martindale, alas, 'can neither stand up to his difficulties nor ignore them' and 'sails over the theory of evolution in a sort of logical balloon flight, with common sense flung overboard for ballast'.

Martindale, a distinguished Jesuit theologian and avid controversialist, was not a man to take this kind of thing lying down, and the correspondence columns of the *New English Weekly* were soon set aflame. Orwell, accused of 'disingenuousness' by his victim, hit back with a letter claiming that 'I think I indicated fairly enough the extent to which he tones down *extra ecclesiam nulla salus* [no salvation outside the Church]'. But the most fascinating consequence of their public disagreement shines out of a recently discovered letter to Eleanor Jaques sent towards the end of July. 'After Father Martindale & I had at each other in print, I had a most interesting interview with him, as he wrote & asked Mrs Carr [a Southwold friend] if I would like to call,' Orwell revealed. Visiting him in London, Orwell found him

very nice & much nicer than his writings, of course & very gifted. We argued for some time, & I would have liked to go on longer, but unfortunately I had to meet someone else. Of course when it came to anything metaphysical I was helpless before him, but I think on some other matters my points told. He told me that the immortality of the soul has been proved beyond possibility of dispute by St Thomas Aquinas, & I must if possible get hold of the passage to see where the hitch is . . .

Not only does the letter shed a revealing light on the young Orwell's attitude to religion (respectful, inquiring, prepared to go out of his way to meet a Catholic theologian who had taken exception to a piece of his writing); it also looks as if it has at least something to do with *Nineteen Eighty-Four*. One can't help noting Orwell's 'helplessness' in the face of this Jesuitical assault and reflecting that O'Brien reduces Winston Smith to an identical state at the Ministry of Love.

◉

Nineteen Eighty-Four ends with Winston successfully reintegrated into the society he has tried to undermine: 'He had won the victory over himself. He loved Big Brother.' But to understand how Winston has reached this point we need to examine Julia's role in the book. Who is she, and what part does she play? Over the years several plausible candidates have been suggested as her original. The most plausible of all is Sonia Brownell, to whom – coincidentally enough – Orwell addressed the very first letter he sent from Jura in April 1947 after returning there to resume work on the novel's first draft.

Julia, when Winston first sets eyes on her, is described as 'a bold-looking girl of about twenty-seven, with thick dark hair, a freckled face and swift, athletic movements. A narrow scarlet sash, emblem of the Junior Anti-Sex League, was wound several times round the waist of her overalls, just tightly enough to bring out the shapeliness of her hips.' In fact, Julia's precise age is later given as twenty-six to Winston's thirty-nine. Sonia at this stage was going on twenty-nine and Orwell nearly forty-four. Something of the confident, if not positively bossy manner that Connolly's *chef du cabinet* brought to her duties at *Horizon* can be glimpsed in Julia's vocal style and her habit of 'bursting' into rooms, but physically Sonia – ash-blonde, Renoiresque and on the plump side – is a rather different proposition. Meanwhile, Julia's 'swift, athletic movements' may recall Brenda Salkeld, who taught gymnastics and games at a girls' private school near Southwold. But the associative net can be drawn wider even than this. Certainly the passage in *Nineteen Eighty-Four* in which Julia tears off her clothes so that her body 'gleamed white in the sun' is reminiscent of one of Orwell's letters to Eleanor Jaques from the early 1930s recalling an idyll in the Suffolk woods. Even Jacintha Buddicom thought that she might have been traduced and complained to a relative many years later that 'At least you have not had the shame of being destroyed in a classic book as Eric did to me.'

None of these identifications is conclusive, and the likelihood is that Julia is a composite of several different women whom Orwell had known over the years. Yet in terms of how *Nineteen Eighty-Four* works as a piece of fiction, all this is of secondary importance to the question of the kind of woman she is. Curiously, Orwell, so precise about Winston's motivation and the factors that have led him to rebel against the Oceanian state, says very little about his co-conspirator. What goes on in her head? With the exception of Winston's speculations about her youth ('She was very young, he thought, she still expected something from life . . . She would not accept it as a law of nature that the individual is always defeated . . . She did not understand that there was no such thing as happiness, that the only victory lay in the far future, long after you were dead'), Orwell never says. We know that she is impulsive, free-spirited and feisty – and as such of enormous figurative significance to a man who has previously had to get by with his mirthless wife Kathleen – but she has little intellectual curiosity, doesn't care for reading and falls asleep when being read to out of *The Principles of Oligarchical Collectivism*.

All this raises a suspicion that Julia is more important for what she symbolises rather than for what she actually is, that her rebellion is merely a case of thwarted hedonism. Elsewhere it is said of her that 'Life as she saw it was quite simple. You wanted a good time; "they", meaning the Party, wanted to stop you having it; you broke the rules as best you could.' But who is she? And how does her relationship with Winston work? Their coming together is clearly her idea: a stumble in the corridor, after which Winston, having helped her to her feet, is slipped a piece of paper bearing the words 'I Love You'. And why has Julia fixed on this unprepossessing older man? Her explanation is surprisingly vague: 'It was something in your face. I thought I'd take a chance. I'm good at spotting people who don't belong. As soon as I saw you I knew you were against *them*.'

Winston, desperate for companionship and the beginnings of an insurrectionary cell, takes this at face value. He seems similarly unperturbed by Julia's revelation that she has a history of seducing – or being seduced by – Party high-ups, the first of whom commits suicide in order to avoid arrest after the affair is discovered. To Winston, even to associate with Julia is tantamount to signing his own death warrant. When they establish a love nest over Mr Charrington's antique shop he reflects that 'Both of them knew that it was lunacy. It was as though they were intentionally stepping nearer to their graves.' On the other hand, when he suggests the plan to Julia, she agrees with 'unexpected readiness'. Julia, it seems clear, is up to something. But what exactly? Some of the most revealing passages about her turn up in the chapter that begins with the disappearance of Syme. Half of her is oddly naïve and uninformed: she has only the faintest idea of who Goldstein is and the doctrines he is supposed to represent. But the other half is ominously sophisticated, tuned in to ideas and deceptions that are beyond Winston's power to comprehend. When on one occasion he mentions the war in Eurasia, she insists that the conflict is simply imaginary and the bombs which fall on Oceania are probably fired by its own rulers 'just to keep people frightened'.

And what does Julia think about rebelling against the Party? We are told that the couple discuss the prospect of active revolt 'but with no notion of how to take the first step'. When Winston tells her of the strange intimacy that he imagines to exist between himself and O'Brien and the impulse he sometimes feels to walk into O'Brien's presence, declare himself the enemy of the Party and ask for help, her response is surprisingly matter-of-fact: 'Curiously, this did not strike her as an impossibly rash thing to do. She was used to judging people by their faces, and it seemed natural to her that Winston should believe O'Brien to be trustworthy on the strength of a single flash of the eyes.' The suspicion that Julia is leading Winston by the nose into O'Brien's clutches is reinforced by the information that, on the morning O'Brien stops Winston in a corridor on the pretext of discussing the latest edition of the Newspeak dictionary, their meeting should take place 'almost at the spot where Julia had slipped the note into his hand'. And it is confirmed by a passage that appears in the original draft of *Nineteen Eighty-Four* but not in the printed text. Here, after Winston and Julia have left O'Brien's flat having been initiated into the workings of a state-wide anti-Party conspiracy, they mysteriously re-encounter each other in the street. Winston is left with 'a curious feeling that although the purpose for which she had waited was to arrange another meeting, the embrace she had given him was intended as some kind of good-bye'. Julia, in other words, is a honey-trap, gamely enticing Winston into O'Brien's lair so that he can be exposed, tormented and ultimately re-educated. From start to finish, you infer, their whole affair is a put-up job.

◎

But if Julia's role in *Nineteen Eighty-Four* is horribly ambiguous, then similar confusions attend the backdrop against which the novel is framed. Technology is everywhere in *Nineteen Eighty-Four*. The real lords of Oceania – Big Brother's henchmen and the zealous enforcers of his will – are architects, designers and engineers: the people responsible for the towering ziggurat of the Ministry of Truth, the telescreen and the military hardware of Airstrip One. The lesson that Orwell took from his dystopian forebears – Wells, Huxley and Zamyatin – with their shimmering concrete skyscrapers and devious experiments in mind control, was that the real power brokers of the future would be technocrats. As he puts it in the essay on James Burnham, the American management guru, the age of the military strongman is in sharp retreat. Tomorrow's world would belong to the managerial class, the inventors, the fixers, the desk-bound power brokers with five-year plans to fulfil and commodities to shift around the globe.

How does this work in practice? The operational landscape of *Nineteen Eighty-Four* is dominated by sophisticated machinery. The telescreen, the chief instrument of state control, is simultaneously the principal weapon of a surveillance culture and a metaphor for the window that the state opens into the consciousness of the average human being. The novel's opening scene, in which Winston sits in his flat in Victory Mansions darkly conscious that his every move is being monitored by persons unseen, assures us that 'there was no way of shutting it off completely'. Any sound beyond the level of a low whisper can be picked up from anyone caught within its field of vision. To extend the range of this 24/7 webcam comes a bugging system so all-encompassing in its sweep that Winston and Julia are forced to meet in the countryside or a secret room to evade its gaze. Even when they wander along a country lane, Julia is still alarmed at the prospect of being eavesdropped on, and, more to the point, being eavesdropped on by someone who knows their identity ('There's always the chance of one of those swine recognising your voice'). And yet, though the novel is crammed with sinister gadgetry, to the point where practically any human interaction can be spied on by unseen eyes, there is almost no indication of how it actually functions.

Take the telescreen. Do you plug it in? Who installs it? What do you do if it goes on the blink? Is there a hotline to call? Who exactly is watching at the other end? The voices that reprimand underperforming exercisers or rebuke misbehaving detainees in the bowels of the Ministry of Love know their targets by name. So does the PT instructress who reprimands Winston for being unable to touch his toes ('6079 Smith W.! Yes, *you*! Bend lower please!'). Unless some extraordinarily sophisticated data-sharer is in charge of the proceedings – and Oceania doesn't seem to run to computers – this suggests that the surveillance is being carried out by teams of screen-watchers, each with a vast bank of individual suspects before them. Orwell notes that 'there was of course no way of knowing whether you were being watched at any given time', while adding that 'It was even conceivable that they watched everybody all the time.' If so, this suggests that, in practical terms, thousands of people must be involved, and that getting on for half the members of the Outer Party must be employed to monitor the activities of the other half.

It is the same with the bugging system, of which Winston and Julia go in perpetual dread. How does it work? How far does its range extend? There is a suggestion that it picks up conversation in the street, so where are the devices installed? Are there drop microphones suspended from street lamps or drones roving overhead? Orwell never says, and so you are left with the spectacle of a surveillance society in which every minor indiscretion is liable to be stamped on by vigilant authority but whose scientific basis is well-nigh unintelligible. As for Winston's day job doctoring back numbers of *The Times*, how exactly is what must be an immensely complex production process carried out? Orwell was writing in the days of hot-metal printing, which would have meant preserving each original plate should anyone want to correct it, so presumably some technological refinements have been introduced. If so, what do they consist of?

The paragraphs that describe Winston at work are oddly vague. He is said to 'dial up' a number on the telescreen and ask for back numbers, after which – at lightning speed – the relevant documents arrive on his desk by way of a pneumatic tube. Once he has dictated his changes into an instrument known as the 'speakwrite', a new version of the edition of the newspaper instantly goes to press. But this process of 'continuous alteration' extends to every means of communication available. It is applied

> not only to newspapers, but to books, periodicals, pamphlets, posters, leaflets, films, soundtracks, cartoons, photographs – to every kind of literature or documentation which might conceivably hold any political or ideological significance. Day by day and almost minute by minute the past was brought up to date.

A programme of these dimensions, which subjects the entire media industry of Oceania to continuous alteration – day by day and minute by minute – would require a vast army of operatives. Who are they? Where do they work? Another obvious need, given all the printing presses and studios working twenty-four hours a day, is almost unlimited cash reserves. Where is the money coming from?

Not, of course, that any of this really matters. Orwell was interested in means, not ends. Throughout *Nineteen Eighty-Four* his angle of attack is moral, not scientific. Yet all this stirs a suspicion that Orwell's imagination is not really animated by the hi-tech, gizmo-ornamented aspects of the future with which science fiction traditionally concerns itself. He is excited (and cast down) by the *idea* of technology and what it can do, but the realities of technological innovation leave him cold. Inevitably, all this goes back to his classical training and an education that put Greek particles ahead of Bunsen burners. No one could accuse Orwell of being a scientific illiterate – he was keen on biology as a teenager, liked dissecting dead birds and knew enough chemistry to concoct a primitive form of gunpowder for the amusement of the small boys he tutored at Southwold. On the other hand, some of his adult engagements with technology are almost breathtaking in their ingenuousness.

One might note, as evidence of this conspicuous detachment from the mechanical basis of the modern world, a jaw-dropping conversation with his friend Richard Rees on the journey from Glasgow to the Gloucestershire sanatorium where he spent the first eight months of 1949. As the train sped south across the English border, Orwell ventured a characteristically ingenuous comment. Was it possible, he wondered, for the trains of one railway company to run on the tracks of another? Or there was the time when, newly arrived at the BBC's Eastern Service in the autumn of 1941 and discovering that the Corporation ran to a 'special effects' department, Orwell is supposed to have immediately rung up the people involved to ask if they could send round 'a good mixed lot', by which he presumably meant a random selection of noises that might come in useful for drama commissions. Few writers have combined such prescience about what technology might do to the world with such a fundamental lack of interest in how technology works.

There is one final puzzle that no close reading of *Nineteen Eighty-Four* can quite ignore. This is its great symbolic bogeyman. Who exactly is Big Brother, beneath whose all-seeing eye the inhabitants of Oceania quail? His poster is on every street corner; he stares from every official announcement; his voice concludes the Two Minutes Hate; and yet the descriptions of him are almost perfunctory. 'The black-moustachio'd face gazed down from every commanding corner.' Elsewhere his face is described as 'black-haired, black-moustachio'd, full of power and mysterious calm'. His expression is peculiarly penetrating. It is not just that 'Big Brother is watching you' but that that the dark eyes in the poster 'looked deep into Winston's own'. His voice, similarly, has no particular register or obvious characteristic. When his on-screen projection begins to speak at the end of a Two Minutes Hate, 'Nobody heard what Big Brother was saying. It was merely a few words of encouragement, the sort of words that are uttered in the din of battle, not distinguished individually but restoring confidence by the fact of being spoken.'

Few other details of Big Brother's appearance, habits or demeanour are vouchsafed. We have no idea of how or when he came by his job, whether he seized power or was voted in by members of the Inner Party. And yet the cult that exists around him is extraordinarily potent. Most of the attendees at the Two Minutes Hate worship him as one might do a god; one woman flings herself at the screen with a cry of what sounds like 'My saviour'. Like Napoleon in *Animal Farm*, he is the fount of all knowledge, the origin of every bright idea. Syme, descanting to Winston on the virtues of Newspeak, is careful to end his account with the gloss 'It was B.B.'s idea originally, of course.' None of this, though, gets us any closer to the reality of Big Brother. When it comes down to it, does he really exist? Winston, enquiring of O'Brien whether Goldstein is a real person, is assured that 'Yes, there is such a person, and he is alive. Where, I don't know.' But what about B.B.? Has he simply been invented to fulfil a need? Will he survive for ever as a propaganda tool-cum-emotional crutch? If so, where does he come from?

As for the figure in the poster, with his black hair, black moustache and expression of 'power and mysterious calm', one might note the famous photograph of Orwell taken in his Islington flat in 1946 by his friend Vernon Richards and the latter's wife Marie-Louise, in which a man with black hair and a black moustache sits staring out at the camera with what could be described as an air of mysterious calm. The designers who assembled the cover of the first American paperback edition of *Nineteen Eighty-Four*, published by Signet Books in 1950, were careful to locate Big Brother in the Cold War politics of the post-1945 era. Targeted at a mass audience, done in flaring colours and with an enticing shoutline ('Forbidden Love . . . Fear . . . Betrayal'), the illustration plainly borrows its inspiration from Hollywood. Winston, much more brooding and muscular than his frail original, bears a faint resemblance to the actor Rock Hudson. Julia, clad in a sleeveless blouse and showing vast amounts of cleavage, looks like a tough baby from the Projects. But Big Brother, his poster glimpsed on the adjoining wall, has clearly not blown in from Burbank. No, despite the addition of some deeply unflattering orc ears, he looks like Stalin.

A still from the 1965 BBC TV dramatisation of Nineteen Eighty-Four.

EPILOGUE: TELLING THE TALE

'A SMOKING ROOM STORY'

Orwell died in the small hours of 21 January 1950 at University College Hospital, London. Three months earlier he had married Sonia Brownell in a ceremony that, given the groom's inability to leave his room, required the issuing of the archbishop of Canterbury's special licence. Close friends noticed that the wedding had a therapeutic effect. Anthony Powell, a frequent visitor, thought that 'In some respects he was in better form there than I had ever known him show.' However, in mid-November Orwell suffered a relapse from which there was no chance of his recovering. The reminiscences of friends who saw him during the last few weeks of his life make for grim reading. He had got so thin, he told one of them, that it was beyond the point at which a human being could hope to survive. He was 'frightful', he warned another, and looked 'like a skeleton'. The last week of his life was spent putting his affairs in order. Three days after he had made his will an exposed artery burst in his lungs: he was dead within a few minutes.

From an early stage it became clear that Orwell's legacy would be the responsibility of his widow. Sonia inherited the bulk of his estate and, with Richard Rees, became his literary executor. It was she who made the decisions about how her late husband's tale would be told. Orwell seems first to have realised that someone might want to write about his life in the wake of *Animal Farm*'s success. 'I don't know if I would, as it were, get up to the point of having anything biographical written about me,' he advised Rees in July 1946, 'but I suppose it could happen and it's ghastly to think of some people doing it.' At this point Orwell appears to have been, if not precisely hostile to an authorised life and times, then prepared to accept the idea if a plausible candidate presented himself. The same letter suggests that 'if someone seems a B.F. [bloody fool], don't let him see any papers'. On the other hand, Orwell also assures Rees that he is going to include among his personal papers 'some short notes about the main events in my life' on the grounds that 'when people write about you, even people who know you well, they always get that kind of thing wrong'.

All this suggests that Orwell was resigned to the prospect of a biography appearing shortly after his death. And yet his will directs that 'no biography of me shall be written'. What was Orwell up to? He seems to have had no objections to biography as a literary form. One of his earliest schemes to break into print in the early 1930s involved a plan to write the life of Mark Twain. Similarly, offered a contract by the firm of Home & Van Thal to produce a biography of George Gissing, he can be found lamenting the fact that an overcrowded schedule prevented him from taking on the work. If Twain and Gissing, why not the author of *Nineteen Eighty-Four*? Whatever Sonia may have thought of this proscription, she did her best to enforce it. Her original scheme was to commission Malcolm Muggeridge to occupy the role of what can only be described as a decoy biographer, the hope being that Muggeridge would commence his work amid great fanfare, take his time and, with luck, never complete the book. In fact, the evidence of Muggeridge's leavings suggests that he spent a fair amount of time on the project throughout the later 1950s, while his official explanation for failing to carry it through – that 'he had found out too much about Orwell that he would rather not have known' – seems faintly disingenuous: in terms of the light it sheds on Orwell's character, none of the material that remains from the Muggeridge project is in the least compromising.

By this juncture, several of Orwell's friends were on the case. Paul Potts's memoir 'Don Quixote on a Bicycle' had appeared in the *London Magazine* in 1957. Together with Dylan Thomas, Eric Gill and Middleton Murry, Orwell is one of the subjects of Rayner Heppenstall's *Four Absentees* (1960). Richard Rees's study, *Fugitive from the Camp of Victory*, which contains eye-witness accounts of Orwell in action and his early career as a journalist, appeared a year later. Sonia's next plan to appease the steadily growing fanbase was an extensive selection of her husband's output, including letters and pieces of minor journalism, which, taken together, would fill in some of the biographical gaps. Collaborating with Ian Angus, then librarian of King's College, London, she spent several years assembling the four-volume *Collected Journalism, Essays and Letters*, which was published in 1968. Still, though, there were siren voices calling for a full-length biography. Infuriated by Peter Stansky and William Abrahams's excellent *The Unknown Orwell* (1972), compiled with no help whatever from the Orwell estate (a sequel, *Orwell: The Transformation*, followed in 1979), she shortly afterwards decided to appoint Bernard Crick, at this point in his career a politics don at Birkbeck College, to write an authorised life.

Crick was a full-time academic, with a newly founded depart-ment to run. Meanwhile, it soon became clear that the project was much more ambitious than he had anticipated. In particular, huge amounts of Orwell's literary journalism still awaited rediscovery in ancient newspaper files. *Orwell: A Life* was eventually published in the autumn of 1980. By this time Crick and Sonia – two highly iras-cible personalities – had fallen out. A piteous letter survives from the previous year to her friend Janetta Parladé in which she complains that 'I was bullied into commissioning a biography of George because people were writing such bad and stupid ones around the place and the person I picked, much abetted by the publisher, has turned out to be quite ghastly'. This is horribly unfair to Crick, who had written a pioneering book, to Secker & Warburg, his publishers, and to Stansky and Abrahams. In Sonia's defence she was by then seriously ill and engaged in a ruinous lawsuit with Orwell's accountants, whom she suspected of siphoning off money from the estate. She died of cancer in December 1980.

Even with Crick and the four-volume *Collected Journalism, Essays and Letters* on the shelves, Orwell Studies was barely in its infancy. W.J. West's discovery in the BBC archive at Caversham of Orwell's wartime broadcasts and news commentaries produced two more fat volumes (*Orwell: The War Broadcasts*, 1985, and *Orwell: The War Commentaries*, 1986). Meanwhile, Secker & Warburg had commissioned an academic named Peter Davison to start work on a project that would transform the Orwell industry for all time. Secker began by asking Davison, primarily known as an Elizabethan textual scholar, if he would be prepared to 'look over' an edition, scheduled for 1984, of the nine full-length books Orwell had published in his lifetime. Out of this grew the mammoth undertaking that became *George Orwell: The Complete Works* (1998). The seventeen years that it took to get all twenty volumes into print were marked by a series of disasters. The first three books did not appear until 1986 and the edition was subsequently abandoned six times. Undeterred by these setbacks, and also by serious ill health – at one point he was forced to undergo a sextuple heart bypass – Davison carried on regardless.

Full of previously unseen letters and journalism quarried from the obscurest of sources, *The Complete Orwell* became the seed corn for several later biographies. Using new material that had become available in the early 2000s – including several eye-opening letters from Orwell's first wife, Eileen – Davison was able to produce a twenty-first volume, *The Lost Orwell* (2006). Further discoveries appeared in his selection from Orwell's writings, *Seeing Things As They Are* (2014).

Even now, the well shows no sign of running dry: two new collections of letters to Orwell's Suffolk girlfriends Eleanor Jaques and Brenda Salkeld were recently purchased by Richard Blair and presented to the Orwell Archive at University College London.

◎

Journalists keen to examine Orwell in the context of twenty-first-century world affairs usually ask two questions: What would Orwell have thought? And: What did Orwell get right? The first is unanswerable. Orwell died nearly three-quarters of a century ago. There is no way of knowing how he might have regarded – to select only three events to which his name is regularly attached – 9/11, the invasion of Iraq or Russia's attack on Ukraine. Anthony Powell, a deep-dyed Conservative, wrote from the perspective of 1983 that 'I think he would have been anti-CND, pro-Falklands Campaign ... and in favour of certain other policies of the Right, which to some extent he always was.' This sounds improbable. But Powell was one of Orwell's closest friends: his views can't simply be dismissed out of hand. In much the same way, more than one pundit surveying the European referendum of 2016 maintained that Orwell would have been broadly in favour of Brexit. Certainly he was an English nationalist (of a sort), with an unshakeable respect for all manner of English tradition, but one of the features of his writing in the immediate post-war era is his recognition of the need for some kind of pan-European alliance, and his essay 'Toward European Unity', published in *Partisan Review* in 1947, argues that the only part of the world in which democratic socialism would have a chance in the near future is Western Europe.

As for what Orwell got right, he regarded *Nineteen Eighty-Four* as a warning rather than a prophecy. All the same, Peter Davison's list of all the novel's predictions that may be said to have come true is worryingly extensive. They include the division of the world into contending zones of influence (not quite in the way that Orwell envisaged, but not too far distant from it either), the emergence of surveillance technology able to subject the most trifling human interaction to detailed scrutiny, environmental degradation, deforestation, the manipulation of language as a way of limiting or subverting our ability to communicate, the mass circulation of pornography and, just for good measure, a National Lottery. The one area in which Orwell doesn't seem to have foreseen our modern arrangements, at any rate in the West, is his insistence that the autocracies of the future would operate in the old-fashioned, tyrannical way. Orwell's Blitz-era review of Huxley's *Brave New World* rebuts its hedonism on the grounds that 'No society of that kind would last more than a couple of generations, because a ruling class that thought principally in terms of a "good time" would soon lose its vitality.' Do the ruling classes of the twenty-first century have 'a strict morality, a quasi-religious view of themselves and a *mystique*'? It seems doubtful. Similarly, it could be argued that Huxley's idea of a future built on technology-based reality-softening is rather closer to the average upper-bourgeois life than the blood, toil and lofted flags of *Nineteen Eighty-Four*.

But in some ways the most fascinating question to be asked of the posthumous Orwell is: What would George have written? Although Orwell left a substantial amount of material that would eventually be published after his death – his war and domestic diaries, the manuscript of 'Such, Such Were the Joys' – his declining health meant that very little work in progress survives from the last year of his life. The essay on Evelyn Waugh was left uncompleted. A long piece which we know he intended to write on Conrad was not even begun. There were also plans for two novels. One of these is mentioned in letters to his American editor Robert Giroux and his friend Tosco Fyvel within a day of each other in April 1949. He told Giroux that he had his next novel 'mapped out' but would not touch it until he felt better. This was a work 'dealing with 1945', Fyvel learned, with the caveat that 'I shouldn't touch it before 1950'. No trace of this survives. What did come to light after Orwell's death, on the other hand, were a few pages of notes for a novella provisionally entitled 'A Smoking Room Story', together with two short drafts of the opening chapter. Orwell's publisher Fred Warburg first heard about it during a visit he paid to the Cotswolds sanatorium in June 1949, from which he reported that it would be 'a novel of character rather than ideas, with Burma as a background'.

Set on the boat returning from Burma in 1927 – the year of Orwell's own journey home – 'A Smoking Room Story' features Curly Johnson, a young man of twenty-four (again, Orwell's age at the time) who has been either sacked or laid off from his job and is, consequently, the butt of unkind remarks from his fellow-passengers: 'Is that the boy who's being sent home?' and so on. The smoking room of the title harbours four Englishmen and four Americans, of whom Orwell's notes observe 'Competition in offensiveness between the two branches of the Anglo-Saxon race – the English worse'. The tone is determinedly realistic. The notes, for example, refer to the newly fashionable short skirts worn by the women on the ship and such popular songs of the day as 'Bye Bye, Blackbird', 'When It's Night-time in Italy' and 'Avalon'. There are also nods to Orwell's own literary tastes in the 1920s, mention of Compton Mackenzie's *Sinister Street* (1913–14) and Margaret Kennedy's *The Constant Nymph* (by which Orwell professed himself bowled over when it was first published in 1924), and talk of Gene Stratton Porter's *A Girl of the Limberlost* (1909), which Dorothy reads to the parish ladies in *A Clergyman's Daughter*.

Here and there, too, in the notes about Curly, come reminders of Flory's apprenticeship in *Burmese Days* ('the dust and squalor of his house, the worn gramophone records, the piled-up whisky bottles, the whores'). Stylistically, 'A Smoking Room Story' has something of that novel's painterly absorption with Far Eastern atmospherics: 'The serang, in his white uniform & scarlet sash, swarmed up the lamp-standard like a monkey, plucked the electric bulb out of the socket, rattled it against his ear to make sure that it was defective, & then tossed it into the foaming wake of the ship. It disappeared &

then broke the water again a hundred yards away, glittering like a diamond.'

And yet what gives the handful of pages their intensely Orwellian flavour is the figurative language, nearly all of which is drawn from the animal world. Curly is said to have soft, curly black hair which clings close to his head and is 'almost like . . . a water-spaniel's coat'. Mr Greenfield of the Indian Civil Service leans against the rail, gazing at the water, 'like some large, harmless animal chewing the cud', and later produces 'the sort of benign, tolerant smile that one might expect to see on the face of some large ruminant animal'. The young people on the boat, of whom Curly is wary, are said to burst out singing 'as spontaneously as a flock of birds'. Mrs Kendrick, the juvenile widow, darts about with movements 'like those of a dragon fly'. We are back in the world of *Keep the Aspidistra Flying* with its anthropomorphised birds, squirrels and lizards. *Animal Farm* and *Nineteen Eighty-Four* are dystopian novels, but here in the year of his death Orwell's work seems to have come full circle. With Curly Johnson on the boat back from Burma, surrounded by his human menagerie, he is reverting to type.

ACKNOWLEDGEMENTS

Warm thanks are extended to Julian Loose, Frazer Martin, Rachael Lonsdale and other members of the Yale team, and to Jacob Blandy for some judicious copy-editing. I should also like to acknowledge the help of the Orwell Estate, in the person of Bill Hamilton of A.M. Heath Ltd, Richard Blair and my agent Gordon Wise. Love, as ever, to Rachel, Felix, Benjy and Leo.

NOTES AND FURTHER READING

The starting point for Orwell Studies is Peter Davison's *George Orwell: The Complete Works* (20 vols, 1998), hereafter *CW*, and its supplement, *The Lost Orwell* (2006). Each of the six full-length biographies by Bernard Crick (1980), Michael Shelden (1991), Jeffrey Meyers (2000), Gordon Bowker (2003) and D.J. Taylor (2003 and 2023) contains useful material. See also John Rodden, ed., *The Cambridge Companion to George Orwell* (2007). Valuable recent studies include Robert Colls, *George Orwell: English Rebel* (2013), John Sutherland, *Orwell's Nose: A Pathological Biography* (2016) and Rebecca Solnit, *Orwell's Roses* (2021). For Orwell's wives, see Sylvia Topp, *Eileen: The Making of George Orwell* (2020) and Hilary Spurling, *The Girl from the Fiction Department: A Portrait of Sonia Orwell* (2002).

Reminiscences of Orwell by those who knew him can be found in Audrey Coppard and Bernard Crick, eds, *Orwell Remembered* (1984) and Stephen Wadhams, ed., *The Orwell Tapes* (new edition, 2017). Also recommended are Richard Rees, *George Orwell: Fugitive from the Camp of Victory* (1961), George Woodcock, *The Crystal Spirit: A Study of George Orwell* (1967), T.R. Fyvel, *George Orwell: A Personal Memoir* (1982) and Anthony Powell, *Infants of the Spring*, vol. 1 of *To Keep the Ball Rolling: The Memoirs of Anthony Powell* (1976), 129–42.

For some contextual background to Orwell's work see Valentine Cunningham, *British Writers of the Thirties* (1988), Andy Croft, *Red Letter Days: British Fiction in the 1930s* (1991) and Benjamin Kohlmann and Matthew Taunton, eds, *A History of 1930s British Literature* (2019).

Most of Orwell's surviving letters and manuscripts may be consulted at the Orwell Archive, University College London. The websites of the Orwell Society (orwellsociety.com) and the Orwell Foundation (orwellfoundation.com) allow access to a wide range of useful material.

Introduction

For reaction to Orwell's death, see Woodcock, *Crystal Spirit*, 45, and Malcolm Muggeridge, *Like It Was: The Diaries* (1982), entry for 26 January 1950. On the long afterlife of *Nineteen Eighty-Four*, see Dorian Lynskey, *The Ministry of Truth: A Biography of George Orwell's 1984* (2019) and D.J. Taylor, *On Nineteen Eighty-Four: A Biography* (2019). Film and TV adaptations are extensively covered in David Ryan, *George Orwell on Screen* (2018). Kingsley Amis, quoted in Blake Morrison, *The Movement: English Poetry and Fiction of the 1950s* (1980), 93.

Rayner Heppenstall, *Four Absentees* (1960), 190. For Jack Bumstead, see D.J. Taylor, 'He Put My Brother in His Book', in Mark Bostridge, ed., *Lives for Sale: Biographers' Tales* (2004), 177–81. Kingsley Amis, 'The Road to Airstrip One', review of Christopher Hollis, *A Study of George Orwell*, *Spectator*, 31 August 1956, reprinted in *The Amis Collection: Selected Non-Fiction 1954–1990* (1990), 96–8. 'The End of Henry Miller', *CW* XIV, *Keeping Our Little Corner Clean: 1942–1943*, 217–19.

1. Heritage

For the review of Rosamund Lehmann, 'The Red-haired Miss Daintreys', *CW* XII, *A Patriot After All: 1940–1941*, 161. Cyril Connolly, *The Evening Colonnade* (1974), 341. The unpublished and undated letter to Eleanor Jaques is in the Orwell Archive at University College London. On seeing Queen Mary's coach, *CW* XIX, *It Is What I Think: 1947–1948*, 25.

Orwell's unfinished essay on Evelyn Waugh and his preparatory notes are in *CW* XX, *Our Job Is to Make Life Worth Living: 1949–1950*, 74–9. For a general survey of Orwell's attitude to religious belief, see Michael G. Brennan, *George Orwell and Religion* (2017). The review of Muggeridge's *The Thirties* is in *CW* XII, 149–52. 'As I Please', *Tribune*, 3 March 1944, *CW* XVI, *I Have Tried to Tell the Truth: 1943–1944*, 113. On Baudelaire, *CW* X, *A Kind of Compulsion: 1903–1936*, 342–3.

Douglas Kerr, *Orwell and Empire* (2022). For background to Orwell's time in Burma, Emma Larkin, *Finding George Orwell in Burma* (revised edition, 2011). Letter to F. Tennyson Jesse, *CW* XVIII, *Smothered under Journalism: 1946*, 126. 'Rudyard Kipling', *CW* XIII, *All Propaganda Is Lies: 1941–1942*, 150–62. On Clarence K. Streit's *Union Now*, *CW* XI, *Facing Unpleasant Facts: 1937–1939*, 358–61.

2. Myths and Legends

For 'Such, Such Were the Joys', *CW* XX, 356–87.

Powell, *Infants*, 136. Heppenstall, *Four Absentees*, 145–6. For P.G. Wodehouse's view of Orwell, Robert McCrum, *Wodehouse: A Life* (2004), 356. Jacintha Buddicom, *Eric & Us* (1974 and revised edition, 2008), *passim*. Letter to Connolly, *CW* XI, 253–4. Letter to Warburg, *CW* XIX, 149–50.

3. Going Native

'Why I Write', *CW* XVIII, 316–21. Dennis Collings in Coppard and Crick, eds, *Orwell Remembered*, 78–9; Ruth Pitter, ibid., 70. For 'La Censure en Angleterre' and 'A Farthing Newspaper', *CW* X, 117–21. 'Hop-Picking Diary', ibid., 214–26, 228–31.

David Astor's memory of Avril, Wadhams, ed., *Orwell Tapes*, 261. Peter Vansittart remembered Orwell's behaviour in pubs in a conversation with the author. For Branthwaite, Wadhams, ed., *Orwell Tapes*, 129.

'Clink', *CW* X, 254–60, 'How the Poor Die', *CW* XVIII, 459–66, 'A Dressed Man and a Naked Man', *CW* X, 322–3.

4. Status Anxiety

The letter to Brenda from 26 June 1931 is in the Orwell Archive. On Orwell's time in Suffolk, Ronald Binns, *Orwell in Southwold* (2018). Letter to Eleanor Jaques of 20 January 1935, Orwell Archive. For the round-up review of dystopian fiction, *CW* XII, 210–13. 'Confessions of a Book Reviewer', *CW* XVIII, 300–2. 'In Defence of the Novel', *CW* X, 517–22.

5. Politics

Letter to Eleanor Jaques of 22 October 1931, Orwell Archive. 'I am against all dictatorships', letter to Michael Sayers, 11 December 1945, Peter Davison, ed., *Orwell: A Life in Letters* (2010). Orwell writes about the socialist meeting in a letter to Brenda of 7 May 1935, *CW* X, 385–7. 'Reams of notes and statistics', ibid., 441–2. *Road to Wigan Pier* diaries, ibid., 417–67.

'He attacked the class barrier . . .', see Alan Sandison, *George Orwell: After 1984* (1986), 197. Philip Mairet, quoted in Crick, *George Orwell: A Life*, 205–6. Fenner Brockway, Wadhams, ed., *Orwell Tapes*, 99–100. For the *New Leader* article, *CW* XI, 167–9. Letter to *New English Weekly*, ibid., 152–4. Herbert Read, ibid., 313–14.

6. Style

'Politics and the English Language', *CW* XVII, *I Belong to the Left: 1945*, 421–32. For the review of *Tropic of Cancer*, *CW* X, 404–5. 'Marrakech', *CW* XI, 416–21.

7. Women

'Liked women to be interesting and intelligent', Kay Ekevall in Coppard and Crick, eds, *Orwell Remembered*, 102. Dennis Collings' comments are taken from the unedited transcript of his contribution to *Orwell Tapes*, accompanying a letter of 4 March 1984 from Stephen Wadhams, Collings papers, Suffolk County Record Office.

'Too cynical or too sardonic', Susannah Collings to author. For Eileen, see Sylvia Topp, *Eileen: The Making of George Orwell* (2020) and Anna Funder, *Wifedom: Mrs Orwell's Invisible Life* (2023). The letter to Brenda Salkeld is in *CW* X, 344–5. For the *Road to Wigan Pier* diary entry, ibid., 427.

8. England

The Lion and the Unicorn, *CW* XII, 392–432. Letter to Dennis and Eleanor Collings of 15 January 1936, Orwell Archive. '. . . a beastly dull country', letter to Connolly, *CW* XI, 253–4. 'Boys' Weeklies', *CW* XII, 57–79. Peter Watson to Connolly, quoted in Clive Fisher, *Cyril Connolly: A Nostalgic Life* (1995), 194. 'Charles Dickens', *CW* XII, 20–57. 'Inside the Whale', ibid., 86–116. 'The Home Guard and You', ibid., 309–12.

The English People: *CW* XVI, *I Have Tried to Tell the Truth: 1943–1944*, 200–28. Letter to Leonard Moore of 6 December 1943, ibid., 17–18. Letter to Gleb Struve of 17 February 1944, ibid., 99. For *Animal Farm* and the Russian Revolution, see Duncan White, *Cold Warriors: Writers Who Waged the Literary Cold War* (2019), *passim* and in particular 164–5. T.S. Eliot, 13 July 1944, *CW* XVI, 282–3. 'For the first time in my life . . .', letter to Gwen O'Shaughnessy of 28 November 1948, *CW* XIX, 475–6.

9. Popular Culture

'The Art of Donald McGill', *CW* XIII, 23–31. 'Decline of the English Murder', *CW* XVIII, 308–10. 'Raffles and Miss Blandish', *CW* XVI, 346–58. Review of *Cricket Country* by Edmund Blunden, ibid., 161–3. 'The Sporting Spirit', *CW* XVII, 440–3. Review of *The Pub and the People*, *CW* XIV, *Two Wasted Years: 1943*, 320–2. 'The Moon Under Water', *CW* XVIII, 98–100.

On Orwell the pub-goer, Humphrey Dakin in Coppard and Crick, eds, *Orwell Remembered*, 128, Woodcock, *Crystal Spirit*, 24–5, and John Morris in Coppard and Crick, eds, *Orwell Remembered*, 173.

10. Big Brother

Letter to Anne Popham of 18 April 1946, *CW* XVIII, 248–51. 'Freedom and Happiness', ibid., 13–16. 'You and the Atom Bomb', *CW* XVII, 323–6. 'Second Thoughts on James Burnham', *CW* XVIII, 268–84, 'The Prevention of Literature', ibid., 370–81.

The account of Orwell's meeting with Father Martindale is based on D.J. Taylor, 'Inside the Catholic Soul', *Tablet*, 20 May 2023. For Jacintha Buddicom and *Nineteen Eighty-Four*, Davison, ed., *Orwell: A Life in Letters*, 8–10. A new edition of the manuscript of *Nineteen Eighty-Four* was published by SP Books (Éditions des Saints Pères) in 2022.

Epilogue: Telling the Tale

'In some respects . . .': Powell, *Infants*, 141. Letter to Rees, *CW* XVIII, 340–1. On Muggeridge as a potential biographer, Richard Ingrams, *Muggeridge: The Biography* (1995), 180. The letter from Sonia to Janetta is in the Orwell Archive. Anthony Powell, *Journals 1982–1986* (1995), 54. 'Toward European Unity', *CW* XIX, 163–7. Letters to Robert Giroux and Tosco Fyvel, *CW* XX, 84–7. Warburg, reporting on a visit to Orwell on 15 June 1949, ibid., 132. 'A Smoking Room Story', ibid., 189–200.

INDEX